Christmas
Handcrafts
Book Two

Oxmoor
House®

Christmas Handcrafts, Book Two

©1993 by Oxmoor House, Inc.
Book Division of Southern Progress Corporation
P.O. Box 2463
Birmingham, Alabama 35201

Published by Oxmoor House, Inc., Leisure Arts, Inc., and Symbol of Excellence Publishers, Inc.

Library of Congress Catalog Card Number: 92-60993
Hardcover ISBN: 0-8487-1135-1
Softcover ISBN: 0-8487-1171-8
Manufactured in the United States of America
First Printing 1993

Oxmoor House, Inc.

Editor-in-Chief: Nancy J. Fitzpatrick
Senior Editor: Mary Kay Culpepper
Editor: Cecilia C. Robinson
Director of Manufacturing: Jerry Higdon
Production Manager: Rick Litton
Associate Production Manager: Theresa L. Beste
Production Assistant: Marianne Jordan

Symbol of Excellence Publishers, Inc.

Editors: Barbara Cockerham, Phyllis Hoffman
Associate Editor: Diane Kennedy-Jackson
Copy Editor: Lorna Reeves
Editorial Assistants: Susan Branch, Cindy Housel, Carol Odom
Production Manager: Wayne Hoffman
Associate Production Manager: Perry James
Creative Director: Mac Jamieson
Art Director: Yukie McLean
Assistant Art Director: Michael Whisenant
Graphic Designers: Scott Begley, Charles Long, Rick Nance
Photography Stylists: Cathy Muir, Tracey M. Runnion

Christmas is the season of memories—memories of holidays past coupled with traditions we love. Such memories inspired this fabulous collection of projects. The flurry of stitching and crafting is at the very heart of the season, so flip through the following pages and begin making some new memories of your own.

Christmas is the season of whispers—whispers of children trying to guess the contents of gaily wrapped packages. What better place to hide small surprises than in a cheery stocking hung from the mantel. There's one for everyone in your family, plus a list of nifty ideas for stocking stuffers.

Christmas is the season of wishing—wishing perhaps for a handmade quilt. The beautiful designs presented are based on traditional patterns and use basic quilting techniques. Make your favorites for soon-to-be heirlooms.

Christmas is the season of love—love for the special people in your life. Use your crafting skills to show them how much you care. From wonderful wearables and ornaments for the tree to festive table settings and other decorations for the home, share your seasonal spirit in every project you complete.

When the last garland is hung, the last package wrapped, and the final cookie baked, may your heart overflow with the joy of Christmas. Enjoy the holidays and linger with family and friends. The best gift you can give is the gift of yourself.

Merry Christmas!

Contents

DAZZLING TREES

Sparkling lights, gleaming tinsel, entwining garlands, and favorite ornaments placed with pride make up memories of your favorite Christmas trees. The tree, traditionally the focal point of the family's seasonal celebration, is placed in a prominent spot in the house, usually one that can be seen from the street! From the moment the lights are wrapped around the branches and turned on, the tree becomes a main attraction at Christmas. It is fitting that tree decorations be presented to inspire your never-ending desire to enhance your tree each year.

For stitchers and crafters, adding new ornaments to an established collection is a favorite part of preparing for Christmas. Whether you have a collection where each ornament is unique, or you have made a dozen of a favorite one, adding to your collection is personal and satisfying. Throughout the pages that follow, there are collections of ornaments to create that will provide hours of enjoyment in the making and years of pleasure as they adorn a holiday tree.

If you feel your ornament collection is complete, perhaps you need to add another tree to your home! Craft enough ornaments to cover a small tree and use it as an accent in your home. Consider a theme tree for your kitchen, library, or sewing room. Suggestions are provided in this chapter for several "specialty" trees, with themes ranging from Victorian to musical.

Make your trees a reflection of you and your family and create new memories each year. Show off your creativity by hosting a Christmas open house and expect rave reviews from your friends.

Country Charm

The Christmas tree is usually a tall, imposing evergreen that reaches from the floor to the ceiling in one corner of the living room. But a smaller version, nestled in an out-of-the-way spot in your kitchen, will add holiday charm to this family gathering area. Here, sparkling lights and this assortment of cross-stitched and handmade ornaments are combined in a picture-perfect tribute to the season. The wax ornaments and dried statice were added to complement the ornaments, and the plaid bow was added for that perfect finishing touch.

No country Christmas tree would be complete without quilted ornaments. Inspired by the *Cathedral Window Quilt* (see page 123), these small ornaments resemble the "windows" of the quilt and are perfect for using tiny fabric scraps left over from major projects. For a dramatic tree, use the same color fabric for the background of your collection and vary the bright colors in the window. For a softer look, use a solid cotton or natural muslin background cloth and fill the windows with a variety of checks or floral prints.

*Above—Simple folding and stitching techniques give these Cathedral Window Ornaments a hand-pieced and quilted look. **Above Right**—Small trees with a sprinkling of handmade ornaments can be tucked into any room and add your personal touch for the holidays.*

Ornaments Galore

Whether your idea of the best holiday tree is one with just a few terrific cross-stitch touches or one that is covered completely with your handwork from the lowest branches to the very tip-top, these designs offer a great variety for crafting and stitching! Some require more time than others and are perfect for autumn stitching when you get the first holiday "bug" and want to get started. Others are quick to do and can be made at the last minute.

Worked with an assortment of vivid floss colors and finished as a decorative tree topper, jolly Saint Nick is certain to find the perfect spot atop your evergreen to watch the festivities, season after season. This cross-stitched Santa will be an endearing part of your holiday decor for years to come.

The combination of a generations-old art form with today's crafting products creates an assortment of unconventional ornaments. Created with Sculpey clay and slick paint, they remind us of the decorated redware clay pieces that were the first pieces of pottery to be produced in the colonies.

If you are a scrap saver, now is the time to get out all of those scraps you have tucked away, waiting for the perfect use, and make an elegant ornament collection. If you have saved lace scraps, beads, and other "dressy" trims, here's your reward—elegant Christmas decorations to craft with your collection of bits and pieces of finery.

The delicate loops and curves of tatting make dainty snowflakes that will hang gracefully from the branches of your tree. The age-old art of tatting is regaining popularity as today's stitchers work to preserve a needlework form more common in their grandmothers' day.

Above—*With just a few passes of the shuttle, timeless treasures can be made. Stiffen them with starch or commercially available fabric stiffener to show off every detail.*

Above—*Make an entire collection of these interesting ornaments to adorn your Christmas tree and combine them with tin ornaments on a fresh evergreen for a warm colonial Christmas.*

Above—*Let your children in on the fun and give them white craft glue, some inexpensive satin-covered balls, and a handful of decorative trims. Watch their eyes sparkle as they create their own holiday masterpieces!*

Above—If you select a fabric other than the one suggested when stitching Saint Nick, be sure your floss covers the fabric with each stitch. It is the densely covered fabric, combined with interfacing, that makes him stand tall on the tree.

Victorian Trimmings

For a decidedly English Christmas, why not make Victorian-style decorations to adorn your tree? Wonderful cross-stitched ornaments take their place among the lace, ribbons, bows, and pearls hung on this lovely tree. Attention to the smallest detail is the key in creating a Victorian Christmas tree, and great care should be taken when selecting the complementary lights, garlands, and glass ornaments. This lavishly decorated pine boasts an array of handmade ornaments, many of which are cross stitched. Whether your favorite is a pastel house, a clock with Roman numerals, or a high-top shoe, complete with pointed toe and six tiny buttons running up the side, you're sure to delight in

stitching them. In addition to providing a new twist on traditional shapes and materials, they also add an oh-so-gentle touch of color with their pastel hues.

Easy-to-make Victorian cones hold yuletide surprises within the branches of this Christmas tree. Made with fabric and lace scraps, they can be color matched to your living room decor. Flowers are a must for adding the final touches to the tree, and the dried bouquet ornaments provide a lovely way to

Right—Pearl roping and glass beads add sparkle to your tree and complement your handmade ornaments. Use soft-white tree lights to give your Victorian tree a warm glow.

Above—Pastel chintz and ivory lace will sit prettily atop any woman's bureau, especially when fashioned into items that hold the owner's favorite baubles. The cones, shown as tree ornaments at right, make perfect containers for little surprises on the tree.

Above—*Miniature bouquets and fans are easy to make and can be made ahead from dried summer blossoms. Even the tiniest scrap of lace and ribbons can be used to decorate these charmers.*

display blossoms preserved from your summer garden.

The finishing touch of dried flowers and lace will complete your elegant Victorian tree. Assorted laces and nosegays are combined to create ornaments that lend a distinctive air to your Christmas tree. The circular lace features an assortment of dried flowers while the fan-shaped ornament uses ribbon flowers with baby's breath. Add the satin ribbon in your favorite color.

13

Above and right—*Crochet is an ageless form of handiwork, and classic pieces like this Welcoming Angel are always in style. Display her as a majestic tree topper, make her the central focus of a tabletop arrangement, or use her to add the perfect seasonal touch to a greenery-laden mantel. Pictured with a pink lining as a tree topper and shown without the lining as a table decoration, the angel creates a delicate silhouette. By simply changing the lining each year, your angel can have a new look.*

Left and below—Not all handmade items require a great deal of time to complete, and these lace ornaments are a classic example. Most of the items needed for this project can be purchased in a local craft store. Plastic foam balls form the foundation. Combine lace doilies, satin ribbon, knee-high hose, and purchased trims, such as the ribbon flowers, miniature bird, or pinecone and nut combination shown here, to make these inexpensive and quick-to-finish gift items.

Above—Delicate stitches worked on fine linen and pinned to plastic foam balls will add your creative touch to the tree this year. Simple, traditional embroidery patterns are easy to stitch. Each ball shown has two panel designs, placed in an alternating fashion. Personalize a ball for each member of the family by stitching his or her monogram on a panel. Include the date as a reminder of a special holiday you've shared.

Hobby Trees

The music of Christmas plays an important role in holiday celebrations. Great renditions of the classics are a part of the season, with tickets purchased months in advance for *The Nutcracker Suite* and plans made to hear the *Messiah* presented again. The anticipation of the performances brings an overwhelming flood of emotion that has been hidden all year. In addition, music speaks to us in the form of a small tinkling bell being rung on a street corner or the lovely church bells in the distance. The excitement of children's voices as they sing out favorite songs of Santa and Rudolph remind us that carols are important to the season. Make this harmonious *Music Tree* as a salute to the musicians, past and present, who make our Christmases so wonderful. Look for old sheet music at garage sales or go through the piano bench and find favorites from your youth to make these wonderful ornaments.

Right—*Gather around the table and share fond memories of your favorite musical moments at Christmas while you and your family make these ornaments. They are quick to craft and will be fun for all.*

17

Sewing leftovers, buttons, pins, and yarn scraps are used to create the ultimate tree for sewing enthusiasts. Wooden spools are given new life as ornaments and buttons do double duty as snowmen. Every decoration on this tree is made with items commonly found in a sewing room. The *Pincushion Ornaments* make wonderful gifts for friends who stitch and can be used after Christmas as a resting place for pins. Let your imagination help you create the tree that truly represents you. If you are lucky enough to have antique laces, experiment with them as garlands for your tree. They will add a delicate touch to the tree and give you a chance to show off your collection. Be sure to keep the lights away from the lace to prevent damage.

Below—The garland, made from sewing cord and gold braid, enhances the collection of ornaments, especially the glass balls decorated with fabric flowers. Save your best floral scraps for these beauties.

Chickadee and Holly

Chickadee and Holly

DMC	Color
● 310	black
・ white	white
7 762	pearl gray, vy. lt.
J 648	beaver gray, lt.
h 646	beaver gray, dk.
3 645	beaver gray, vy. dk.
O 3033	mocha, vy. lt.
c 3347	yellow-green, med.
+ 3346	hunter
z 3345	hunter, dk.
e 347	salmon, dk.
L 3328	salmon, med.
◢ 433	brown, med.
bs 3348	yellow-green, lt.
bs 801	coffee, dk.
bs 221	pink, dk.

Fabric: 18-count smoke Aida
Stitch count: 41H x 45W
Design size:

11-count	3¾" x 4⅛"
14-count	3" x 3¼"
18-count	2¼" x 2⅓"
22-count	1⅞" x 2⅛"

Instructions: Cross stitch using two strands of floss. Backstitch using one strand of floss.

Backstitch (bs) instructions:

—	3348
‖‖‖	310
••••	801
⌒⌒⌒	646
••••	221

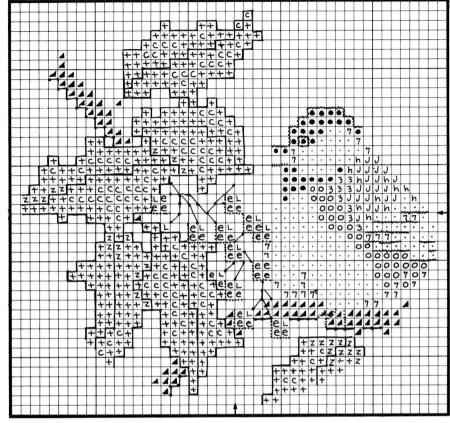

CHICKADEE AND HOLLY

Yellow Tabby Cat

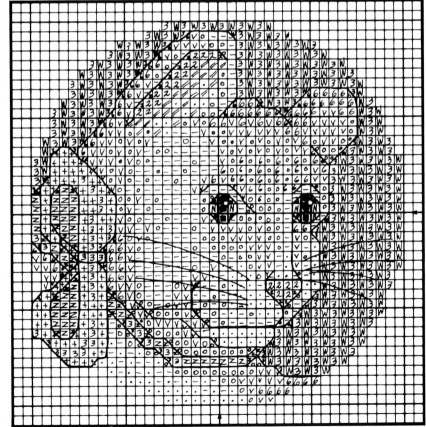

YELLOW TABBY CAT

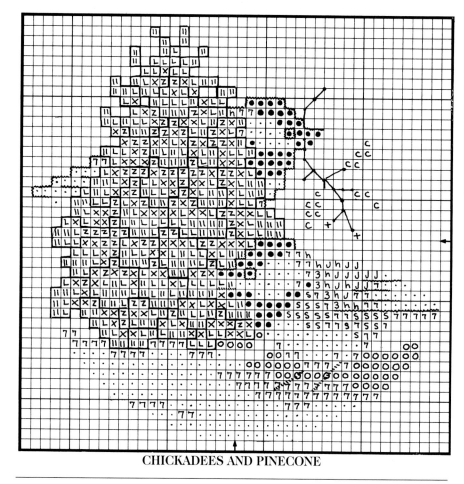

CHICKADEES AND PINECONE

Chickadees and Pinecone

Yellow Tabby Cat

	DMC	Color
●	white	white
-	3078	golden yellow, vy. lt.
	white	white
o	725	topaz
	3078	golden yellow, vy. lt.
v	725	topaz
6	783	gold
	782	topaz, med.
■	310	black
N	562	jade, med.
z	498	red, dk.
3	304	red, med.
+	321	red
w	699	green
2	760	salmon
∕	761	salmon, lt.
	white	white
bs	3328	salmon, med.
bs	780	topaz, vy. dk.

Fabric: 27-count white Linda Cloth by Zweigart®

Stitch count: 40H x 40W
Design size:

14-count	2⅞" x 2⅞"
18-count	2¼" x 2¼"
22-count	1⅞" x 1⅞"
27-count	3" x 3"

Instructions: Cross stitch over two threads, using two strands of floss. Backstitch using one strand of floss unless otherwise indicated. Straight stitch using one strand of white for whiskers (stitch last). When two colors are bracketed together, use one strand of each.

Backstitch (bs) instructions (stitch in order listed):

310	eyeballs
white	dot in each eye (two strands)
3328	mouth, around nose
498	ribbon around neck
699	bow
780	outer edges of cat, ears, eyebrows, chin, and bridge of nose

Chickadees and Pinecone

	DMC	Color
●	310	black
X	801	coffee, dk.
z	898	coffee brown, vy. dk.
L	433	brown, med.
‖	435	brown, vy. lt.
·	white	white
7	762	pearl gray, vy. lt.
J	648	beaver gray, lt.
h	646	beaver gray, dk.
3	645	beaver gray, vy. dk.
s	3033	mocha, vy. lt.
O	3022	brown-gray, med.
c	3347	yellow-green, med.
+	347	salmon, dk.
bs	3345	hunter, dk.

Fabric: 18-count smoke Aida
Stitch count: 41H x 40W
Design size:

11-count	3¾" x 3⅝"
14-count	3" x 2⅞"
18-count	2¼" x 2"
22-count	1⅞" x 1¾"

Instructions: Cross stitch using two strands of floss. Backstitch using one strand of floss.

Backstitch (bs) instructions:

—	433
∿∿	646
‖‖‖	310
····	3345

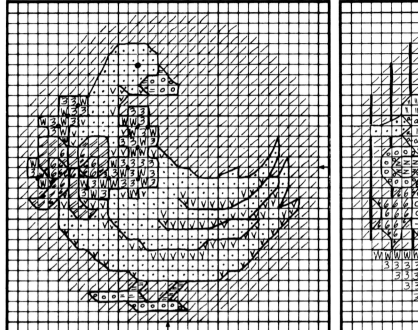

CHRISTMAS GOOSE

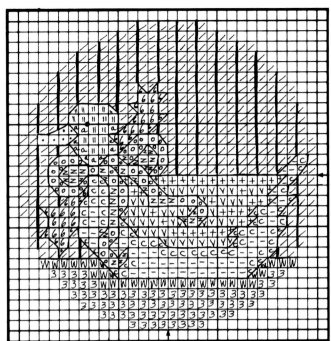

MALLARD

Christmas Goose

DMC	Color
╱ 930	antique blue, dk.
• white	white
V 762	pearl gray, vy. lt.
o 742	tangerine, lt.
= 741	tangerine, med.
W 890	pistachio, ul. dk.
3 367	pistachio, dk.
‖ 304	red, med.
6 498	red, dk.
bs 939	navy, vy. dk.

Fabric: 25-count pewter or white Lugana from Zweigart®
Stitch count: 30H x 30W
Design size:

14-count	2¼" x 2¼"
18-count	1⅝" x 1⅝"
22-count	1⅜" x 1⅜"
25-count	2⅓" x 2⅓"

Instructions: Cross stitch over two threads, using two strands of floss. Backstitch (bs) using one strand 939. Make French knots using two strands of 304 for berries and 939 for eyes of goose where • appears at intersecting grid lines, wrapping floss around needle once.

Christmas Goose

Mallard

Mallard

DMC	Color
a 469	avocado
‖ 470	avocado, lt.
• 742	tangerine, lt.
W 938	coffee, ul. dk.
3 801	coffee, dk.
- 739	tan, ul. lt.
C 738	tan, vy. lt.
+ 433	brown, med.
V 434	brown, lt.
o 304	red, med.
z 498	red, dk.
6 890	pistachio, ul. dk.
╱ 3078	golden yellow, vy. lt.
bs 3371	black-brown

Fabric: 14-count Fiddler's Lite from Charles Craft, Inc.
Stitch count: 30H x 30W
Design size:

11-count	2¾" x 2¾"
14-count	2¼" x 2¼"
18-count	1⅝" x 1⅝"
22-count	1⅜" x 1⅜"

Instructions: Cross stitch using two strands of floss. Backstitch (bs) using one strand 3371. Make French knots for eyes where • appears at intersecting grid lines, using two strands 3371 and wrapping floss around needle twice.

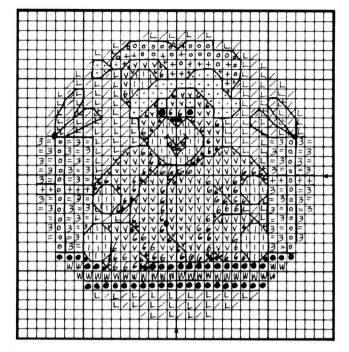

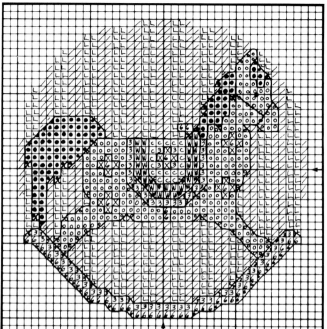

TEDDY'S FIRST CHRISTMAS

ROCKING HORSE

Teddy's First Christmas

DMC	Color
· white	white
/ 727	topaz, vy. lt.
L 726	topaz, lt.
= 320	pistachio, med.
3 319	pistachio, vy. dk.
o 321	red
+ 304	red, med.
● 3371	black-brown
W 801	coffee, dk.
6 435	brown, vy. lt.
V 436	tan
I 739	tan, ul. lt.

Fabric: 14-count Fiddler's Lite from Charles Craft, Inc.
Stitch count: 30H x 30W
Design size:

11-count	2¾" x 2¾"
14-count	2¼" x 2¼"
18-count	1¾" x 1¾"
22-count	1⅓" x 1⅓"

Instructions: Cross stitch using two strands of floss. Backstitch using one strand of floss unless otherwise indicated. Make French knots where ● appears at intersecting grid lines, using two strands of floss and wrapping floss around needle twice.
Backstitch (bs) instructions:
321   bows (two strands)
3371   all other backstitch
French knots:
321   base of bows on packages
3371   teddy's belly button

Rocking Horse

Teddy's First Christmas

Rocking Horse

DMC	Color
● 310	black
o 745	yellow, lt. pl.
/ 746	off white
L 564	jade, vy. lt.
6 350	coral, med.
3 351	coral
C 352	coral, lt.
W 561	jade, vy. dk.
X 562	jade, med.

Fabric: 30-count unbleached linen from Norden Crafts
Stitch count: 40H x 40W
Design size:

14-count	2⅞" x 2⅞"
18-count	2¼" x 2¼"
22-count	1⅞" x 1⅞"
30-count	2¾" x 2¾"

Instructions: Cross stitch over two threads, using two strands of floss. Backstitch using one strand 310. Straight stitch using one strand 561 for bridle. Make French knots for eye where ● appears at intersecting grid lines, using two strands 310 and wrapping floss around needle twice.

Cathedral Window Ornaments

Materials:
Assorted fabric squares (**Note:** A 2" square is required for **each** ornament.)
10" length ¼"-wide complementary satin ribbon (for **each** ornament)
Muslin (for backing ornaments) (**Note:** A 2" square is required for **each** ornament.)
Thread to match muslin and ribbon
Measuring tape
Hand-sewing needle
Scissors
Pencil

1. Using 2"-square cardboard pattern from quilt (refer to instructions for *Cathedral Window Quilt*, page 140), cut one fabric square for each ornament you wish to make.
2. Cut 5"-square pattern from cardboard and lightly trace around pattern on muslin. Cut out muslin backing pieces.
3. Find and mark center of each 5" muslin square. Press ¼" hem on all four sides. Fold each corner to center and press folds, making sure each corner comes to sharp point.
4. Place one 2" fabric square in center of each folded piece. Fold edges of muslin over square and appliqué folds.
5. Tie 10"-length ribbon into bow and tack at top center of each ornament, using matching thread.
6. Thread needle with 7" length thread to match muslin, stitch through top of each ornament, and tie knot in thread ends to form hanger.

Tatted Star and Snowflake

Abbreviations:	
ch—chain	**prev**—previous
cl—close ring	**r**—ring
ds—double stitch	**rw**—reverse work
j—join	**sp**—small picot
p—picot	

Finished Sizes: Star measures 4"; snowflake measures 4⅓".

Materials:
14 yds. size 20 white crochet thread
Small steel crochet hook
Tatting shuttle   Scissors
Fabric stiffener   Plastic wrap

Beginning at base of point with ball and shuttle—
*r:12ds, sp, 3ds, (p, 3ds) 3 times, cl, rw.

ch: 4ds, (p, 4ds) 3 times, rw.
r: 12ds, sp, 3ds, (p, 3ds) 3 times, cl, rw.
ch: 3ds, (p, 3ds) 4 times.
r: 3ds, j to last p of prev ch, 3ds, (p, 3ds) 4 times, cl.
ch: 3ds, j to last p of prev r, 3ds, (p, 3ds) 3 times, j to sp of opposite r; ch: 4ds, (p, 4ds) 3 times, rw.
r: 3ds, (p, 3ds) 3 times, j to center sp of opposite r, 12ds, cl.
Repeat from * four times for star or five times for snowflake. Tie thread in base of first r and cut ends. Stiffen, following manufacturer's instructions. Place on plastic wrap and let dry thoroughly. To form hanger, cut 7" length of thread, pass one end through top of point, and tie thread ends together.

Redware Hearts

Materials:
Sculpey clay, 2-oz. pkg. **each**, colors: #032 orange, #082 red, #552 brown (**Note:** Makes 6–8 ornaments.)
Small heart cookie cutter
1 tube yellow slick paint (available in craft stores)
Paper clips (for hangers)
Waxed paper   Ruler
Cookie sheet   Plastic wrap
Rolling pin
Wire cutters
Heavy paper (optional, for pattern)
Craft knife (optional)

Option: If desired, use photo below to make heart-shaped pattern from heavy paper and use craft knife to cut shapes from clay.
Note: ALWAYS wash hands before working with clay and be sure hands are dry before beginning. Soften clay by kneading it thoroughly with hands until it is soft and pliable. Create new colors by kneading separate colors together until completely blended. Roll out clay between sheets of waxed paper. Wrap extra clay tightly in plastic wrap to store.

1. Using wire cutters, snip smaller loop off each paper clip to make hanger for each ornament.
2. Mix clay colors together until thoroughly blended, using six parts orange, six parts brown, and one part red Sculpey clay. Roll out between sheets of waxed paper to 3/16" thick. Cut out heart shapes with cookie cutter or use pattern to trace heart shapes onto clay. Cut out using craft knife. Re-roll leftover clay and cut out more hearts.
3. Lay hearts on cookie sheet and insert paper clip loop in 3/16" edge at top center of each heart. Bake at 300° F for fifteen minutes. Remove from oven and let cool.
4. Paint with slick paint, using photo on page 10 and design motifs as a guide. Let paint dry completely before moving.

Dried Bouquet Ornaments

Materials:
18" length 3"-wide white lace
1 yd. ¼"-wide mauve ribbon
Baby's breath, colors: white, mauve
Dried roses
Dried pink globe amaranths
Pressed fern leaves
Thread to match lace
Hand-sewing needle
Scissors
Measuring tape   Fabric stiffener
Paintbrush   Aluminum foil
Cardboard   Hot glue gun

Note: Materials listed will make one *Dried Bouquet Ornament*.

1. Cover cardboard with aluminum foil. Set aside.
2. Run gathering thread close to edge of lace along lengthwise edge. Sew short ends of lace together and pull gathering thread, forming a circle. Place circle of lace on foil-covered cardboard and paint with fabric stiffener. Let dry overnight.
3. Glue roses and amaranths in center of lace circle. Fill in with leaves and baby's breath.
4. Cut two 3"-long streamers from ribbon. Place one end of each streamer under nosegay and glue in place. Use remaining ribbon to make ribbon bow, looping ribbon back and forth and tacking in center to secure. Glue ribbon bow to lace, placing at top of streamers.
5. Thread needle with 7" length thread, stitch through top of ornament, and tie knot in thread ends to form hanger.

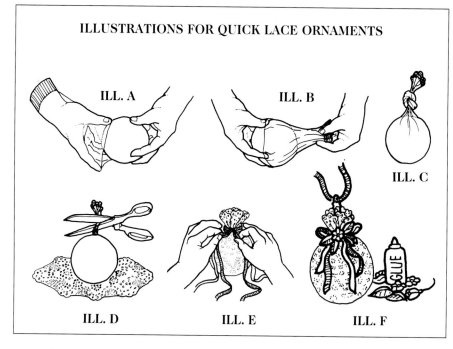

ILLUSTRATIONS FOR QUICK LACE ORNAMENTS

ILL. A

ILL. B

ILL. C

ILL. D

ILL. E

ILL. F

Quick Lace Ornaments

Materials:
One 3" STYROFOAM brand plastic foam ball
One colored knee-high stocking
One 14" purchased crochet doily
Three ¾-yd. lengths ¼"-wide satin ribbon to complement stocking color
Assorted silk leaves, flowers, and decorative trims
Scissors
Extra-long hairpin
Hot glue gun **or** fabric glue **or** long straight pins

Note: Materials listed will make one *Quick Lace Ornament.*

1. Put hand in knee-high stocking, reaching all the way to toe.
2. Grasp Styrofoam® ball through stocking, referring to Illustration A, and pull stocking off hand and over ball, referring to Illustration B.
3. Tie top of stocking in knot close to surface of ball, referring to Illustration C. Trim excess stocking off above knot, referring to Illustration D.
4. Place stocking-covered ball in center of doily with knot on top, again referring to Illustration D.
5. Gather doily around ball, pulling toward knot at top. Secure by tying with two pieces ribbon, referring to Illustration E. Tie tightly with bow knots. Trim ribbon ends to desired length.
6. Use hot glue gun or fabric glue to secure assorted leaves, flowers, and/or other decorative items. Let cool or dry completely.

Note: If you wish to preserve doily, use long straight pins instead of glue.
7. Push long hairpin into top of Styrofoam® ball, leaving a loop at top and referring to Illustration F.
8. Thread remaining piece of ribbon through hairpin loop, referring to Illustration F. Determine desired hanging length and tie ribbon ends in a bow to form hanging loop.
Note: If ornaments are hung closely, vary lengths of hanging loops for variety.

Music Room Tree

Note: For these projects, a general materials list has been given. Specific materials for each project have been listed separately.

General materials:
7" length metallic gold thread for **each** ornament (for hanger)
Paintbrushes, sizes: ⅓"-wide, ¼"-wide
Scissors   Ruler

Sheet Music Ornaments
Materials:
2⅓" STYROFOAM brand plastic foam ball for **each** ornament
4" piece wire covered with white fabric for **each** ornament
Sheet music   Mod Podge®
8" length ¼"-wide red satin ribbon for **each** ornament (optional)

1. Bend fabric-covered wire in half and stick ends into Styrofoam® ball. Twist top of wire to form loop for thread hanger.

2. Tear sheet music into small pieces. Apply Mod Podge® to back side of each piece with ⅓"-wide paintbrush, press onto ball with brush, and apply more Mod Podge®, pressing piece of music smooth against ball. Continue process, overlapping each piece, until ball is completely covered. Let dry.
3. Apply four to five coats Mod Podge® over entire ball, letting dry between coats.
4. Thread 7" length gold thread through loop and tie knot in thread ends to form hanger.
Option: Trim top of ornament with ribbon bow tied through loop.
5. Repeat for remaining ornaments.

Plastic Instrument Ornaments
Materials:
Purchased white plastic instrument ornaments
Pearl Finish by Cerameoat®

1. Remove hangers from purchased Plas-Ztie® ornaments.
2. Apply two to three coats Pearl Finish by Cerameoat® to each ornament, using ¼"-wide paintbrush and letting dry between coats.
3. Thread 7" length gold thread through each ornament and tie knot in thread ends to form hanger.

Decorated Ball Ornaments
Materials:
2⅓" purchased clear glass ball ornaments
9 ft. purchased gold musical garland
Tacky glue

1. Cut notes and other musical motifs from one end of garland. Glue as desired on clear glass ball.
2. Thread 7" length gold thread through hanger loop and tie knot in thread ends to form hanger.
3. Repeat for remaining ornaments.

Plaid Bows
Materials:
1⅓ yds. ¾"-wide red-and-black plaid ribbon for **each** bow
6" piece red pipe cleaner for **each** bow (for securing center)
Note: Lay ruler flat on work surface for measuring. You will need both hands to hold ribbon.

1. To make first streamer, measure 3" of ribbon (**DO NOT CUT**) and crimp edges together at this point. This crimped area will be center of bow.
2. To make first loop, hold crimped area between thumb and forefinger, with right side facing you. Measure 4" of remaining ribbon, bring to back of center,

crimp edges together, and twist ribbon so right side is up. This loop will be to left of bow's center.

Note: Each time you bring loop to center, you must twist ribbon so that right side will be up for next loop.

3. To make second loop, continue to hold center as indicated. Measure 4" of remaining ribbon, bring to back of center, crimp edges together and twist ribbon over so right side of ribbon is up. This loop will be to right of bow's center.

4. Continue making loops on left and right of bow's center until there are five loops on either side. Always bring crimped ribbon to back of bow.

5. Let second streamer stick out with right side facing you.

6. Secure center of bow (crimped area) with pipe cleaner, twisting tightly. **DO NOT CUT PIPE CLEANER ENDS.**

7. Beginning on one side of center, pull one loop up and one loop down until each loop is in a pleasing position. Repeat for other side.

8. Trim ends of streamers and tie bow to tree using pipe cleaner ends.

9. Repeat for remaining bows.

Musical Note Ornaments
Materials:
3" x 4" piece balsa wood for **each** ornament (available at craft stores)
Red acrylic paint
Water-base satin varnish
Pencil and paper
Small nail
Hammer
Scroll saw

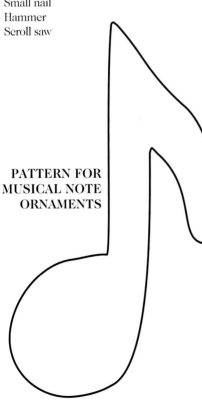

PATTERN FOR MUSICAL NOTE ORNAMENTS

1. Trace pattern onto paper, cut out, and place on wood. Draw around pattern and saw out note using scroll saw. Use hammer and nail to make small hole in top of note for hanger.

2. Paint note with two coats red acrylic paint, using ⅓"-wide paintbrush and letting dry between coats. When dry, apply two coats water-base satin varnish, letting dry between coats and after second coat.

3. Thread 7" length gold thread through hole in top of note and tie knot in thread ends to form hanger.

4. Repeat for remaining ornaments.

Sewing Room Tree

Note: For these projects, a general materials list has been given. Specific materials for each project have been listed separately.

General materials:
7" length metallic gold thread for **each** ornament (for hanger)
Measuring tape
Scissors
Tacky glue

Decorated Glass Ball Ornaments
Materials:
2⅓" purchased glass ball ornaments
Assorted print fabric scraps

1. Cut motifs from fabric scraps and glue to glass ball ornaments, placing as desired.

2. Thread 7" length gold thread through hanger loop and tie knot in thread ends to form hanger.

3. Repeat for remaining ornaments.

Pincushion Basket Ornaments
Materials:
Purchased miniature baskets
Assorted fabric scraps
Thread to match fabric scraps
Polyester filling
Straight pins with colored heads
Hand-sewing needle

1. Cut a circle from fabric approximately 1⅓" larger than diameter of basket.

2. Run gathering thread around circle ¼" in from edge of fabric. Pull thread to gather fabric edges together, stuffing fabric center with polyester filling to form ball. Secure thread.

3. Glue ball into basket.

4. Glue ends of 7" length gold thread to opposite sides of basket.

5. Stick pins into pincushion.

6. Repeat for remaining ornaments.

Button Ornaments
Materials:
Assorted buttons, ¾"–1" in diameter
8–9 small safety pins for **each** ornament

1. Place button face down on flat work surface. Dip "hinge" ends of safety pins into glue and press onto back side of button, spacing evenly. Let dry.

2. Thread 7" length gold thread through one safety pin and tie knot in thread ends to form hanger.

3. Repeat for remaining ornaments.

Spool Ornaments
Materials:
Small empty wooden spools
18"–20" lengths embroidery floss in assorted colors

1. Bring ends of 7" length gold thread together and glue ends in hole of empty spool to form hanger. Let dry.

2. Wrap length of embroidery floss around spool, securing first end under wrapped floss and gluing remaining end to spool. Let dry.

3. Repeat for remaining ornaments.

Decorative Cord
Materials:
60"–90" lengths ¼" white cord
80"–110" lengths ⅛"-wide metallic gold braid

1. Glue braid around cord, following direction of twist in cord. Let dry.

2. Drape on tree.

Lace Ornaments
Materials:
Assorted 12"-long lace trim scraps
Thread to match
Assorted pairs of buttons
Hand-sewing needle

1. Run gathering thread along one lengthwise edge of lace scrap. Overlap short ends and baste together. Gather lengthwise edge to form circle. Secure thread.

2. Glue button on either side of lace circle at center, covering thread.

3. Thread needle with 7" length gold thread, stitch through hole in edge of lace, and tie knot in thread ends to form hanger.

4. Repeat for remaining ornaments.

Button Snowmen Ornaments
Materials:
3 white buttons of same style, sizes: small, medium, large, for **each** ornament
5" length ⅛"-wide green satin ribbon for **each** ornament
Permanent black marker
Small scrap red felt   Hand-sewing needle

1. Overlap edge of small button atop edge of medium button and glue in place. Overlap edge of medium button atop edge of large button and glue in place. Let dry.

2. Draw on eyes, nose, mouth, and buttons, using black permanent marker and referring to photo on page 18.

3. Tie ribbon around snowman's neck (where small and medium buttons are glued together) to make scarf. Freehand draw small hat on red felt, referring to photo. Cut out hat and glue to top of snowman's head.

4. Thread needle with 7" length gold thread, stitch through top of hat, and tie knot in thread ends to form hanger.

5. Repeat for remaining ornaments.

Knitting Yarn Angel Ornaments
Materials:
1" STYROFOAM brand plastic foam ball for **each** ornament
12 yds. white yarn for **each** ornament
4" x 6" length white lace for **each** ornament
4⅓" x 8" piece cardboard
4"-square piece cardboard

1. To make head, wrap yarn around Styrofoam® ball, gluing as you go.

2. To make body, cut length of yarn eight yards long and wrap around 4⅓" side of cardboard. Cut 5" length of yarn and tie wrapped yarn together at top of cardboard to form neck. Slip yarn off cardboard and lay flat on work surface. To make arms, wrap three yards yarn around 4"-square piece cardboard. Slip off cardboard. To make hands, tie length of yarn approximately ⅓" from end of each arm and trim loops. Slip arms through body near neck. Tie length of yarn around body, directly under arms, to hold them in place. Glue head to body.

3. To make wings, fold lace into pleats and tie in center with yarn. Glue to back of angel.

4. Thread needle with 7" length gold thread, stitch through back of angel's head, and tie knot in thread ends to form hanger.

5. Repeat for remaining ornaments.

Welcoming Angel

```
Crochet Abbreviations:
beg—begin(ning)        st(s)—stitch(es)
bet—between            tr—triple crochet
ch(s)—chain(s)         yo—yarn over
dc—double crochet      =—equal to or
dec—decrease               count as
hdc—half double        rep—repeat * to *
    crochet                number of
lp(s)—loop(s)              times
nxt—next                   indicated
sc—single crochet      "V" sp—dc, ch,
sk—skip                    and dc
sl st—slip stitch          all in the
sp(s)—space(s)             same sp
```

```
Crochet Terms:
Link: To make a link, ch 3 and dc in the sp
bet the last ch 3 and dc.
Note: Links are a fast, easy way to cover
distance with airy, yet solid stitches.
Marker: Place dark removable thread or
safety pin to aid in counting stitches or
finding future location. Count stitches and
mark key rows as you work. At beg of row,
ch 2 counts as sc, ch 3 counts as dc.
```

Materials:
225 yds. ivory bedspread thread (**Note:** DMC's ecru Baroque was used for model.)
Size 8 steel crochet hook
15"-tall x 4" STYROFOAM brand plastic foam cone
Approximately 9 cotton balls (for stuffing head)
Dark sewing thread **or** safety pin
Hand-sewing needle (if using sewing thread)
Fabric stiffener   **Rustproof** pins
Waxed paper   Plastic wrap
Rubber band   Scissors   Foam board
¼ yd. 44/45"-wide fabric of your choice (optional, for lining)

Note: Materials listed will make one *Welcoming Angel.*

Head
Ch 4, sl st in first ch to form ring.
Row 1: Ch 2, make 7 sc in ring (= 8 sc). Sl st in ch-2.
Row 2: Ch 2 (place marker), 2 sc in nxt sc. *Sc in nxt sc, 2 sc in nxt sc.* Rep from * around (= 12 sc). Sl st in ch-2.
Row 3: Ch 3 (move marker), 2 dc in nxt sc. *Dc in nxt sc, 2 dc in nxt sc.* Rep from * around (= 18 dc). Sl st in ch-3.
Row 4: Ch 3, 2 dc in nxt dc. *Dc in nxt dc, 2 dc in nxt dc.* Rep from * around (=27 dc). Sl st in ch-3.
Rows 5–9: Ch 3, dc in each dc around (= 27 dc). Sl st in ch-3. At end of rows 9, 12, and 16, insert cotton balls into head and neck.

Chin and Neck
[To dec, insert hook in st, yo, pull lp through st (= 2 lps on hook), insert hook in nxt st, yo, pull lp through st (= 3 lps on hook), yo, pull thread through all 3 lps on hook.]
Rows 10–11: Ch 2, *dec 1 st, sc in nxt 2 sts.* Rep from * around until you have 20 sc and 15 sc. Sl st in ch-2.
Row 12: Ch 2, *dec 1 st, sc in nxt st.* Rep from * around (= 10 sc). Sl st in ch-2.
Rows 13–15: Ch 2, sc in each sc (= 10 sc). Sl st in ch-2.

Cape
Row 16: Ch 2, sc in sl st. *2 sc in nxt sc.* Rep from * around (= 20 sc). Sl st in ch-2.
Row 17: Ch 2, sc in each sc **and** make 2 sc in every 5th sc around (= 24 sc). Sl st in ch-2 (remove marker).

Bodice
Row 18: Sc in sl st. *Ch 3, sk 1 sc, sc in nxt sc.* Rep from * around except instead of final sc make sl st in first sc and ch (= 12 sps).
Row 19: Sc in sp. *Ch 4, sc in nxt sp.* Rep from * around except instead of final sc make sl st in first sc and nxt sp. (Place marker in center ch-4 sp in back to beg halo later.)
Row 20: Ch 4, in same sp make dc, ch 1, dc, ch 1. *In nxt sp make dc, ch 1, dc, ch 1, dc, ch 1.* Rep from * around, sl st in third ch and nxt sp.
Row 21: Ch 3, dc in same sp, ch 1, in nxt sp make 2 dc, ch 1. *Sk 1 sp, in each of nxt 2 ch-1 sps make 2 dc, ch 1.* Rep from * around, sl st in ch-3.
Row 22: Ch 3, dc in nxt dc, ch 1, dc in nxt 2 dc, ch 2. *Dc in nxt 2 dc, ch 1, dc in nxt 2 dc, ch 2.* Rep from * around, sl st in ch 3. (Fill head and neck, if necessary with cotton balls.)

Skirt
Row 23: Ch 4, dc in nxt dc, ch 2. *Dc in nxt dc, ch 1, dc in nxt dc, ch 2.* Rep from * 4 times. Sk 12 dc, fold right-side out. Rep from * 6 times more, sl st in 3rd ch, sp, dc and sp (= 12 ch-2 sp).
Row 24: Ch 4, dc in same ch-2 sp, ch 3, sc in nxt ch-2 sp, ch 3. *In nxt ch-2 sp make dc, ch 1, dc (= "V" sp); ch 3, sc in nxt ch-2 sp, ch 3.* Rep from * around, sl st in third ch and sp (6 "V" sp).
Row 25: Ch 4, dc in same sp, ch 4. *In nxt "V" sp make dc, ch 1, dc, ch 4.* Rep from * around, sl st in 3rd ch and sp.
Row 26: Ch 4, dc in same sp, ch 3, sc in nxt sp, ch 3. *In nxt "V" sp make dc, ch 1, dc; ch 3, sc in nxt sp, ch 3.* Rep from * around, sl st in third ch and sp.
Rows 27–28: As rows 25 and 26.
Row 29: Ch 4, in same sp make dc, ch 1, dc, ch 4. *In nxt "V" sp make dc, ch 1, dc, ch 1, dc, ch 4.* Rep from * around, sl st in third ch and sp.
Row 30: Ch 4, dc in same sp, in nxt "V" sp make dc, ch 1, dc (beg 2 "V" sps per panel). Ch 3, sc in nxt sp, ch 3. *In each of nxt 2 ch-1 sps make dc, ch 1, dc; ch 3, sc in nxt sp, ch 3.* Rep from * around, sl st in third ch and sp.
Row 31: Ch 4, dc in same sp, sk 2 dc, in nxt "V" sp make dc, ch 1, dc, ch 5. *In each of nxt 2 "V" sps make dc, ch 1, dc; ch 5.* Rep from * around, sl st in third ch and sp.
Rows 32–35: As rows 30–31.
Row 36: Ch 4, dc in same sp, ch 1, in nxt "V" sp make dc, ch 1, dc; in nxt sp make ch 3, sc, ch 3, sc, ch 3 (place marker). *In each of nxt 2 "V" sps make dc, ch 1, dc with ch 1 bet "V" sps; in nxt sp make ch 3, sc, ch 3, sc, ch 3.* Rep from * around, sl st in third ch and sp.
Row 37: Ch 4, dc in same sp, ch 1, in nxt "V" sp make dc, ch 1, dc, ch 5. *In each of nxt 2 "V" sps make dc, ch 1, dc with ch 1 bet "V" sps, ch 5.* Rep from * around, sl st in third ch and sp.
Rows 38–39: As rows 36–37.

Rows 40–43: As rows 36–37, except make ch 2 instead of ch 1 bet "V" sps with ch 1 still in "V" sp in panels.

Rows 44–45: Rep rows 36–37 but ch 5 to beg row and make ch 2 instead of ch 1 bet "V" sp and ch 2 in "V" sps in panels.

Rows 46–47: As rows 44–45, except make ch 3 bet "V" sps.

Rows 48–49: As rows 44–45, except make ch 4 bet "V" sps.

Rows 50 (advance marker)–53: Rep rows 44–45 but ch 5 bet "V" sps.

Row 54: Ch 5, dc in same sp, in nxt sp make ch 3, sc, ch 3. *In nxt "V" sp make dc, ch 2, dc; in nxt sp make ch 3, sc, ch 3, sc, ch 3; in nxt "V" sp make dc, ch 2, dc; in nxt sp make ch 3, sc, ch 3.* Rep from * around, sl st in third ch and sp.

Row 55: As row 53.

Rows 56–57: As rows 54 and 53.

Skirt Edging

Row 58: Ch 5, dc in same sp; in nxt sp make ch 3, sc, ch 2, sc, ch 3. *In nxt "V" sp make dc, ch 2, dc; in nxt sp make ch 3, sc, ch 2, sc, ch 3.* Rep from * around, sl st in third ch and sp.

Row 59: Ch 5, dc in same sp, ch 3. *In nxt ch-2 sp make dc, ch 2, dc, ch 3.* Rep from * around, sl st in third ch and sp (= 24 "V" sps).

Rows 60–61: As row 59. Fasten off.

Right Sleeve

With back facing, attach thread on row 22 in first dc of armhole after ch-2 sp.

Row 1: Ch 5, tr in nxt dc. *Ch 2, dc in nxt dc, ch 1, dc in nxt dc.* Rep from * to * 3 times. Ch 2, tr in nxt dc, ch 1, tr in nxt dc; ch 2, tr in nxt dc which is same underarm dc as skirt in front, ch 1, tr in same underarm dc as skirt in back; ch 2, sl st in fourth ch and sp (counting beg sp and underarm set = 7 ch-1 sps).

Row 2: Ch 5, tr in same sp, ch 3, sc in nxt sp, ch 3; in nxt ch-1 sp make tr, ch 1, tr; ch 3, sc in nxt sp, ch 3. *In nxt ch-1 sp make dc, ch 1, dc; ch 3, sc in nxt sp, ch 3.* Rep from * to * once. *In nxt ch-1 sp make tr, ch 1, tr; ch 3, sc in nxt sp, ch 3.* Rep from * to * once. In nxt ch-1 sp at underarm make tr, ch 1, tr, ch 3, sc in nxt sp, ch 3, sl st in fourth ch and sp (= 7 ch-1 "V" sps).

Row 3: Ch 5, tr in same sp; ch 4, in nxt ch-1 "V" sp make tr, ch 1, tr, ch 4. *In nxt "V" sp make dc, ch 1, dc, ch 4.* Rep from * once. *In nxt "V" sp make tr, ch 1, tr, ch 4.* Rep from * to * 2 times, sl st in fourth ch and sp (= 7 "V" sps).

Row 4: Ch 5, tr in same sp; in nxt sp make ch 3, sc, ch 3; in nxt "V" sp make tr, ch 1, tr; in nxt sp make ch 3, sc, ch 3. *In nxt "V" sp make dc, ch 1, dc; in nxt sp make ch 3, sc, ch 3.* Rep from * once. * In nxt "V" sp make tr, ch 1, tr; in nxt sp make ch 3, sc, ch 3.* Rep from * 2 times, sl st in fourth ch and sp.

Row 5: Rep row 3 except make ch 5 instead of ch 4 bet "V" sps.

Row 6: Ch 6, tr in same sp; in nxt sp make ch 3, sc, ch 2, sc, ch 3; in nxt "V" sp make dc, ch 2, dc; in nxt sp make ch 3, sc, ch 2, sc, ch 3. *In nxt "V" sp make sc, ch 2, sc; in nxt sp make ch 3, sc, ch 2, sc, ch 3.* Rep from * to * once. In nxt "V" sp make dc, ch 2, dc; in nxt sp make ch 3, sc, ch 2, sc, ch 3. *In nxt "V" sp make tr, ch 2, tr; in nxt sp make ch 3, sc, ch 2, sc, ch 3.* Rep from * to * once, sl st in fourth ch and sp (= 14 ch-2 sps).

Row 7: Ch 6, tr in same sp, ch 3; in nxt ch-2 sp make tr, ch 2, tr, ch 3; in each of nxt 2 ch-2 sps make dc, ch 2, dc, ch 3; in each of nxt 3 ch-2 sps make sc, ch 2, sc, ch 3; in each of nxt 2 ch-2 sps make dc, ch 2, dc, ch 3; in each of nxt 5 ch-2 sps make tr, ch 2, tr, ch 3; sl st in fourth ch and sp (= 7 tr, 4 dc and 3 sc "V" sps).

Row 8: As row 7.

Row 9: Rep row 7 except make ch 4 instead of ch 3 bet "V" sps. Fasten off.

Left Sleeve

With front facing, make to match right sleeve.

Halo

With back facing, find center ch-4 sp in row 19; attach thread to sc on right.

Row 1: Ch 3, dc in same sc. *Ch 3, dc in sp bet last ch-3 and dc.* Rep from * to * 10 times (= 12 links). Ch 13, dc in third ch from hook, make 11 ch-3/dc links. Without twisting row 1, sl st in sc to left center to correspond with right side (= 12 links on each side).

Row 2: Ch 1, turn, sl st in dc side of last link. Ch 4, turn, sc in ch-1 sp on row 20. Ch 1, turn, in same link make 2 tr. Into dc side in each of nxt 2 links make 3 tr; in each of nxt 3 links make 3 dc; in each of nxt 3 links make 3 hdc; in each of nxt 3 links make 3 sc; sc in each ch across. Make other side to match with 3 sc, hdc, dc, and tr. Sc in corresponding ch-1 sp on row 20 (3 dc in bet). Continue with right wing.

Right Wing

With thread still attached at end of halo on right shoulder, work rows 1, 3, and 5 in sp DOWN sides of skirt panel.

Row 1: *Ch 8, dc in sp below on nxt row.* Rep from * to * once. Ch 8, dc in sc on nxt row; ch 4, tr in sc on nxt row (= 4 sps).

Row 2: Turn. *Ch 8, tr in nxt ch-8 sp.* Rep from * to * 2 times; ch 6, sk 5 tr, tr in nxt tr; ch 8, sk 5 sts, dc in nxt dc. Ch 8, sk 5 sts, sc in nxt dc. Ch 8, sk 5 sts, sl st in nxt 4 hdc (= 7 sps).

Row 3: Turn. *Ch 8, sc in nxt ch-8 sp.* Rep from * to * once. Ch 8, dc in nxt sp. *Ch 8, tr in nxt sp.* Rep from * to * 4 times, tr in sc on nxt row (= 9 sps).

Row 4: Turn. *Ch 8, tr in nxt sp.* Rep from * to * 4 times. Ch 8, dc in nxt sp. *Ch 8, sc in nxt sp.* Rep from * to * once. Ch 8, sk 3 sc, sl st in nxt 4 sc (= 9 sps).

Row 5: Turn. *Ch 8, sc in nxt sp.* Rep from * to * 2 times. *Ch 8, dc in nxt sp.* Rep from * to * 6 times. Ch 4, sc in sc on nxt row (=11 sps). Fasten off here for RIGHT wing.

Left Wing

With back facing, attach thread at halo in corner tr.

Rows 1–5: As for right wing, except do NOT cut thread after row 5. On row 6 make edge around BOTH wings in a continuous row.

Wing Edging—Row 6: Ch 3, turn, dc in last dc. In each of nxt 4 ch-8 sps make 8 dc, dc in dc; in each of nxt 3 sps make 8 hdc, hdc in dc or sc; in each of nxt 3 sps make 8 sc, sc in sc, sc in 2 sc. Sl st in each st across top and make edge on other side to match with sp and st, 2 sc; 3 sps with sc; 3 sps with hdc; 4 sps with dc; ch 3, sl st in same sc as at end of row 5. Fasten off.

To stiffen:

Saturate all but head in fabric stiffener or two-to-one solution of fresh white glue and water. Protect head with plastic wrap and rubber band at neck. Gently squeeze out excess. Insert plastic foam cone wrapped in waxed paper into skirt. Make lines of crochet straight. Flute skirt edge. Lay angel on back on waxed paper atop foam board with skirt edge below board edge. Shape and pin wings and halo with RUSTPROOF pins. Arrange sleeves and head. When ALMOST DRY, remove pins and cone. Stand angel upright and arrange into desired position. Finish drying and shape head.

Note: Use fan or hair dryer to speed drying.

To line:

To line skirt, trim plastic foam cone to 9⅓". Wrap cone with fabric, trim edges of fabric, and glue to secure. Place inside stiffened angel. To line sleeves, lightly cover 3" x 6" piece matching fabric with fabric stiffener and place sticky side down atop waxed paper. Let dry. Trace around sleeve pattern and cut two pieces. Make a fold on dotted line from points A to C with waxed paper to inside. Insert lining into sleeve, placing point C at shoulder.

SLEEVE PATTERN

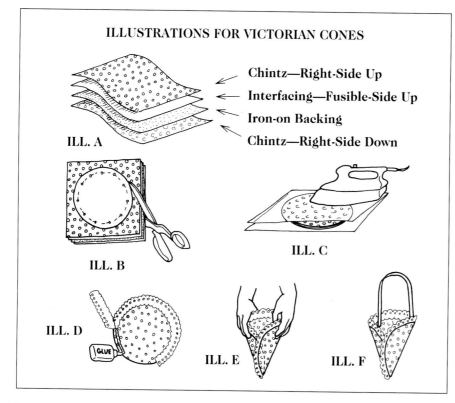

ILLUSTRATIONS FOR VICTORIAN CONES

Chintz—Right-Side Up
Interfacing—Fusible-Side Up
Iron-on Backing
Chintz—Right-Side Down

ILL. A

ILL. B

ILL. C

ILL. D

GLUE

ILL. E

ILL. F

Victorian Cones

Materials:
Two 7"-square pieces chintz fabric
7"-square piece iron-on backing
7"-square piece fusible interfacing
11" length ⅜"-wide ivory satin ribbon
15⅓" length ¾"-wide gathered ivory lace
Kraft paper **or** brown paper bag
Nonstick pressing sheet
Fabric glue
Straight pins
Scissors   Measuring tape
Waxed paper   Compass
Pencil   Iron

Note: Materials listed will make one *Victorian Cone.*

1. Preheat iron to wool setting.
2. To make pattern for fabric and fusing, draw 6"-diameter circle on kraft paper, using compass and pencil.
3. Layer chintz (right-side down), iron-on backing, interfacing (fusible-side up), and chintz (right-side up), referring to Illustration A. Pin pattern atop top layer of chintz, pinning through all layers. Cut out, referring to Illustration B. Remove pins and paper pattern, being careful to keep fabric, backing, interfacing, and fabric stacked together.
4. Place cut, stacked pieces inside folded, nonstick pressing sheet, referring to Illustration C. Press for approximately 10 seconds. Let cool. Turn and repeat on reverse side. Remove stacked, fused circle from pressing sheet and

place atop flat work surface, placing sheet of waxed paper between fused circle and work surface.
5. Glue lace approximately ⅛" in from edge of fused circle on what will be outside of cone, using fabric glue and referring to Illustration D.
Note: Lace will not reach all the way around circle.
6. Bring edges of circle together to form ice-cream cone shape, referring to Illustration E and making sure portion of circle with lace overlaps portion without lace.
7. Glue cone where circle overlaps. Use glue generously and hold in place several minutes until glue sets.
8. Dab glue on one end of satin ribbon at least 1⅓" in from end. Place halfway between front and back of cone on inside of cone, referring to Illustration F. Hold until glue sets. Let dry. Repeat on other side.

Trimmed Ornaments

Materials:
Purchased white satin-covered ornaments
Assorted white laces, trims, pearl beads, sequins, etc.
Craft glue
Scissors

1. Glue assorted laces, trims, pearl beads, sequins, etc., to satin-covered ornaments, placing as desired.
2. Let dry.

Lace Fans with Roses Ornaments

Materials:
9" length 7"-wide ecru lace
Scraps of mauve taffeta, cut 6" x 4" for large bud and 4" x 2⅓" for small bud
1 yd. ¼"-wide green satin ribbon
Dried **or** silk rose leaves
Baby's breath, colors: white, mauve
Thread to match lace
Hand-sewing needle
Scissors
Measuring tape
Fabric stiffener
Aluminum foil
Cardboard
Florist's tape
Pliable wire, cut into 3"–4" lengths
Wire cutters
Hot glue gun

Note: Materials listed will make one *Lace Fan with Roses* ornament.

Making fans:
1. Cover cardboard with aluminum foil. Set aside.
2. Gather lace 1⅓" from bottom edge and tack to secure.
3. Dip lace into fabric stiffener. Run lace between two fingers to squeeze out excess fabric stiffener. **DO NOT WRING.** Place lace on foil-covered cardboard. Work with lace to form the shape of a fan, pinching in pleats to simulate the folds of a fan. Let dry overnight.

Making roses:
1. Fold taffeta in half along lengthwise edge. Fold one corner over, forming a triangle. Roll fabric to form a bud, gathering at base of bud as you go. Approximately 1" from end of fabric, fold raw edges down. Wrap wire around base of bud ¼" from bottom.
2. Wrap base of bud and wire with florist's tape. (This will become stem.)

Finishing:
1. Join buds to rose leaf, using florist's tape and rolling tape around bottom of stem to secure.
2. Glue buds to fan, centering atop tacked area at bottom of fan.
3. Make a ribbon bow, looping ribbon back and forth and tacking in center to secure. Glue at base of buds. Glue on baby's breath, placing as desired.
4. Thread needle with 7" length thread, stitch through center top of fan, and tie knot in thread ends to form hanger.

Victorian Cross-Stitch Ornaments

Materials:
⅓ yd. 44/45"-wide complementary fabric (for backing)
8" length ⅜"-wide complementary satin ribbon (for **each** ornament)
Thread to match fabric
Polyester filling
Hand-sewing needle
Scissors   Measuring tape
Sewing machine (optional)

1. Complete cross stitch following instructions given.
2. Place completed cross-stitch design on backing fabric to determine size piece backing fabric needed. Cut out backing fabric.
3. Center completed cross-stitch design wrong-side up atop right side of backing material.
4. Machine- or hand-sew around perimeter of ornament, using edge of cross-stitch design as a guide and leaving 2" opening at top for turning.

5. Trim seam allowance to ¼". Clip corners and curves.
6. Turn ornament right-side out and stuff lightly with polyester filling. Whipstitch opening closed, tacking ribbon hanging loop at top center of ornament as you stitch.
7. Repeat 1–6 for remaining ornaments.

TEAPOT

Teapot

	DMC	Color
C	676	old gold, lt.
Z	729	old gold, med.
O	3687	mauve
V	3688	mauve, med.
╱	712	cream
X	739	tan, ul. lt.
3	827	blue, vy. lt.
L	522	fern green
S	523	fern green, lt.
bs	520	fern green, dk.
bs	680	old gold, dk.

Fabric: 14-count ecru Aida
Stitch count: 58H x 85W
Design size:

11-count	5¼" x 7¾"
14-count	4⅛" x 6"
18-count	3¼" x 4¾"
22-count	2⅝" x 3⅞"

Instructions: Cross stitch using three strands of floss. Backstitch using two strands of floss.

Backstitch (bs) instructions:
•••• 520   stems of flowers and leaves
— 680   teapot

29

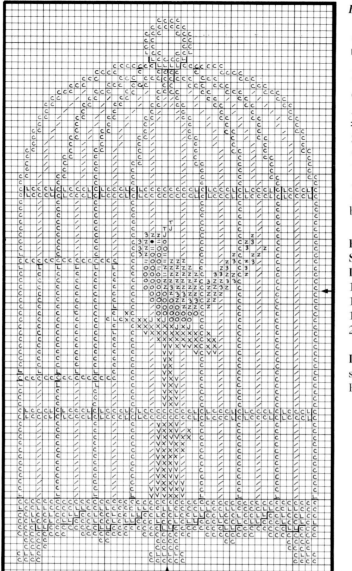

Bird in a Cage

DMC	Color
C 729	old gold, med.
L 680	old gold, dk.
X 522	fern green
V 520	fern green, dk.
O ecru	ecru
Z 826	blue, med.
= 827	blue, vy. lt.
3 825	blue, dk.
● 310	black
T 3687	mauve
J 3688	mauve, med.
∕ 676	old gold, lt. (two strands)
bs 420	hazelnut, dk.

Fabric: 14-count rose Aida
Stitch count: 84H x 48W
Design size:

11-count	7⅝" x 4⅜"
14-count	6" x 3⅓"
18-count	4⅝" x 2⅝"
22-count	3⅞" x 2¼"

Instructions: Cross stitch using three strands of floss, unless otherwise indicated. Backstitch (bs) using two strands 420.

BIRD IN A CAGE

CHRISTMAS JOY

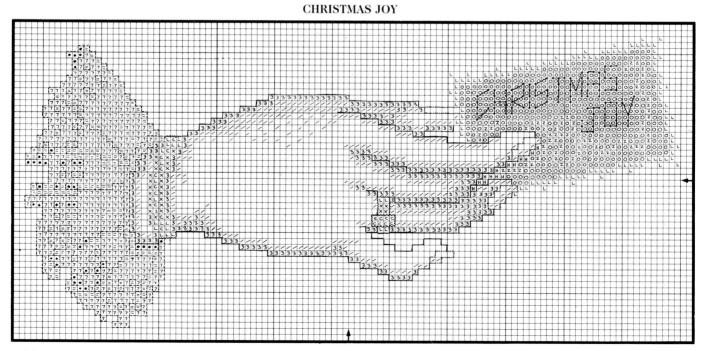

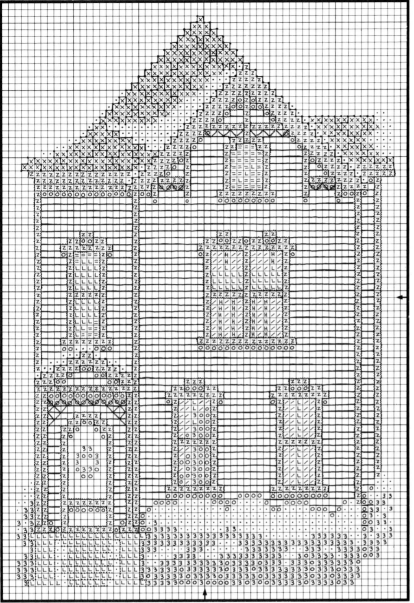

GREEN HOUSE

Green House

	DMC	Color
·	white	white
X	898	coffee brown, vy. dk.
Z	3689	mauve, lt.
o	522	fern green
3	520	fern green, dk.
L	415	pearl gray
/	ecru	ecru
H	822	beige-gray, lt.
=	318	steel gray, lt.
bs	3371	black-brown
bs	3688	mauve, med.
bs	414	steel gray, dk.

Fabric: 14-count aspen green Aida
Stitch count: 85H x 58W
Design size:

11-count	7¾" x 5¼"
14-count	6" x 4⅛"
18-count	4¾" x 3¼"
22-count	3⅞" x 2⅝"

Instructions: Cross stitch using three strands of floss. Backstitch using two strands of floss.

Backstitch (bs) instructions:
- ···· 3371   roof, top of door
- — 522   horizontal lines of house
- ∿∿ 3688   house outline
- ···· 414   steps, concrete pedestals

Christmas Joy

	DMC	Color
X	729	old gold, med.
L	680	old gold, dk.
o	712	cream
Z	520	fern green, dk.
/	951	flesh, vy. lt.
3	950	flesh, lt.
H	822	beige-gray, lt.
C	825	blue, dk.
=	3023	brown-gray, lt.
7	3024	brown-gray, vy. lt.
•	3022	brown-gray, med.
bs	3064	flesh, med.
bs	221	pink, dk.

Fabric: 18-count blush Aida
Stitch count: 49H x 113W
Design size:

11-count	4⅜" x 10¼"
14-count	3⅓" x 8⅛"
18-count	2¾" x 6¼"
22-count	2¼" x 5⅛"

Instructions: Cross stitch using three strands of floss. Backstitch using two strands of floss, unless otherwise indicated.

Backstitch (bs) instructions:
- — 3064   (one strand)
- ‖‖‖ 950   fingertips
- ···· 221   lettering
- ∿∿ 729   ring
- ···· 3022   cuff (one strand)

Pocket Watch

	DMC	Color
L	676	old gold, lt.
o	729	old gold, med.
Z	680	old gold, dk.
V	3687	mauve
H	520	fern green, dk.
bs	420	hazelnut, dk.

Fabric: 14-count ecru Aida
Stitch count: 80H x 66W
Design size:

11-count	7¼" x 6"
14-count	5¾" x 4¾"
18-count	4⅓" x 3⅝"
22-count	3⅝" x 3"

Instructions: Cross stitch using three strands of floss. Backstitch using two strands of floss.

Backstitch (bs) instructions:

∿∿	420	watch stem
—	520	Roman numerals
‖‖‖	3687	points on clock hands
····	680	*CHRISTMAS*, design under *XII*

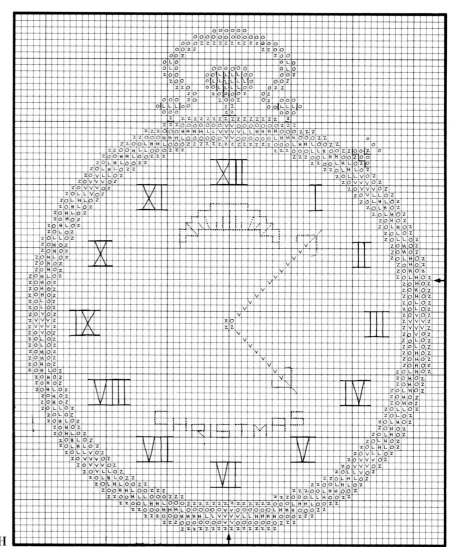

POCKET WATCH

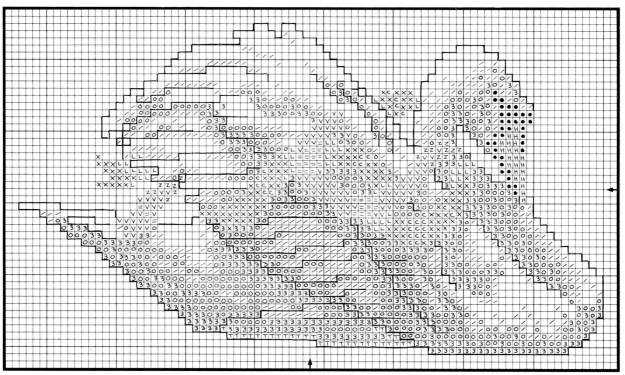

GRACEFUL SWAN

CITY CHRISTMAS

City Christmas

	DMC	Color
•	white	white
C	523	fern green, lt.
X	522	fern green
V	224	pink, lt.
L	415	pearl gray
Z	318	steel gray, lt.
3	520	fern green, dk.
O	317	pewter gray
S	524	fern green, vy. lt.
=	827	blue, vy. lt.
7	221	pink, dk.
H	729	old gold, med.
bs	223	pink, med.

Fabric: 14-count rose Aida
Stitch count: 84H x 57W
Design size:

11-count	7¾" x 5¼"
14-count	6" x 4⅛"
18-count	4¾" x 3⅛"
22-count	3⅞" x 3⅝"

Instructions: Cross stitch using three strands of floss. Backstitch using two strands of floss.

Backstitch (bs) instructions:

∿∿∿	522	house outline
—	223	horizontal lines in house
‖‖‖‖	317	roof, above door, top door panels
••••	318	window panes, concrete pedestals, lower door panels, wreath

Graceful Swan

	DMC	Color
C	524	fern green, vy. lt.
X	523	fern green, lt.
L	522	fern green
=	225	pink, vy. lt.
V	224	pink, lt.
Z	223	pink, med.
●	310	black
╱	3047	yellow-beige, lt.
O	3046	yellow-beige, med.
3	3045	yellow-beige, dk.
T	420	hazelnut, dk.
H	977	gold-brown, lt.

Fabric: 14-count ecru Aida
Stitch count: 46H x 84W
Design size:

11-count	4⅛" x 7⅓"
14-count	3¼" x 6"
18-count	2⅓" x 4¾"
22-count	2⅛" x 3⅞"

Instructions: Cross stitch using three strands of floss. Backstitch using two strands 420.

Embroidered Ball Ornaments

High-Top Shoe

	DMC	Color
O	3688	mauve, med.
Z	3687	mauve
C	ecru	ecru
V	543	beige-brown, ul. lt.
X	523	fern green, lt.
L	828	blue, ul. lt.
□	224	pink, lt.
3	676	old gold, lt.

Fabric: 14-count rose Aida
Stitch count: 84H x 62W
Design size:

11-count	7¾" x 5⅝"
14-count	6" x 4⅓"
18-count	4¾" x 3⅓"
22-count	3⅞" x 2¾"

Instructions: Cross stitch using three strands of floss. Backstitch using two strands 224. Where ● appears, stitch tiny buttons or pearls.

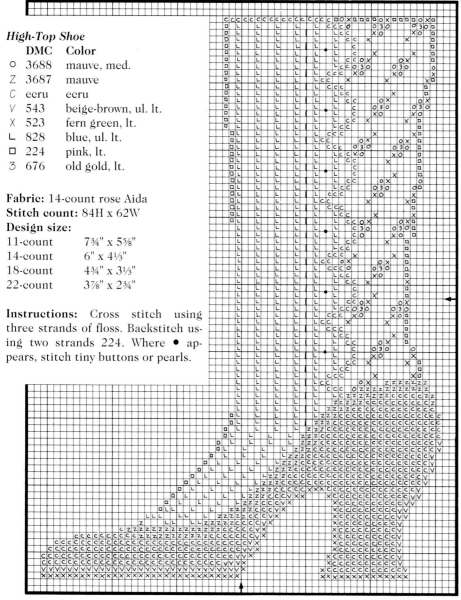

HIGH-TOP SHOE

Materials:
3⅓" STYROFOAM brand plastic foam ball
1⅓ yds. ⅜"-wide satin ribbon in color to match floss used
6" x 18" piece linen
Small embroidery hoop
Straight pins   Metal screw eye
Graphite paper   Craft glue
Tracing paper   Pencil
Hand-sewing needle Scissors
Measuring tape

Note: Materials listed will make one *Embroidered Ball Ornament*. Four sets of designs (one large design and one small design) are given. One set was used for each ornament.

1. Trace panel pattern onto tracing paper twice. Select design set (large and small) of your choice and center each design inside traced panel pattern. Trace design. Position on bias of linen fabric, placing graphite paper between design and linen. Trace each complete design onto linen twice.
2. Place fabric in hoop and embroider design, using colors and stitches indicated in color code for design you are working.
3. Cut along traced outside edge of panel pattern and pin fabric pieces to Styrofoam® ball, alternating large and small designs and placing pins near edge of fabric.
4. Beginning at top and working around ball back to top, glue ribbon over pins.
5. Cut four 4"-long pieces from remainder of ribbon. Glue ends together and glue ends to center top, aligning with ribbon previously wrapped around perimeter of ornament.
6. Insert metal screw eye into top center of ornament. Thread remaining ribbon through screw eye and tie ends together to form hanger.

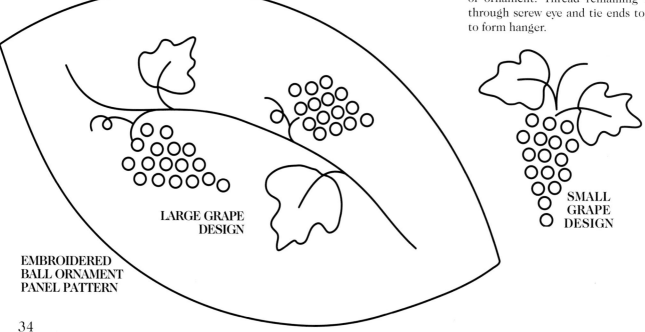

LARGE GRAPE DESIGN

SMALL GRAPE DESIGN

EMBROIDERED BALL ORNAMENT PANEL PATTERN

Holly Ball

DMC	Color
3345	hunter, dk.
3052	green-gray, med.
304	red, med.

Instructions: Make stitches using one strand of floss. Make French knots using two strands of floss, wrapping floss around needle once.

Outline stitch instructions:

3345	holly stems and leaves
3052	pine stems
304	outline of ribbon (one strand)

Satin stitch instructions:

304	holly berries on small design, ribbon

French knot instructions:

304	holly berries on large design

Lazy daisy instructions:

3052	pine needles

Mauve Flower Ball

DMC	Color
3727	mauve, lt.
3726	mauve, med. lt.
745	yellow, lt. pl.
3053	green-gray

Instructions: Make stitches us-ing two strands of floss. Make French knot using two strands of floss, wrapping floss around needle twice.

Outline stitch instructions:

3053	stems

Satin stitch instructions:

3727	flowers
3726	flower buds
3053	leaves
745	center of flowers

French knot instructions:

3726	small buds on tendril

Grape Ball

DMC	Color
3041	antique violet, med.
501	blue green, dk.
831	olive, med.

Instructions: Satin stitch using one strand of floss unless otherwise indicated. Outline stitch using one strand of floss unless otherwise indicated.

Satin stitch instructions:

3041	grapes
501	leaves (two strands)

Outline stitch instructions:

501	stems (two strands)
831	tendrils

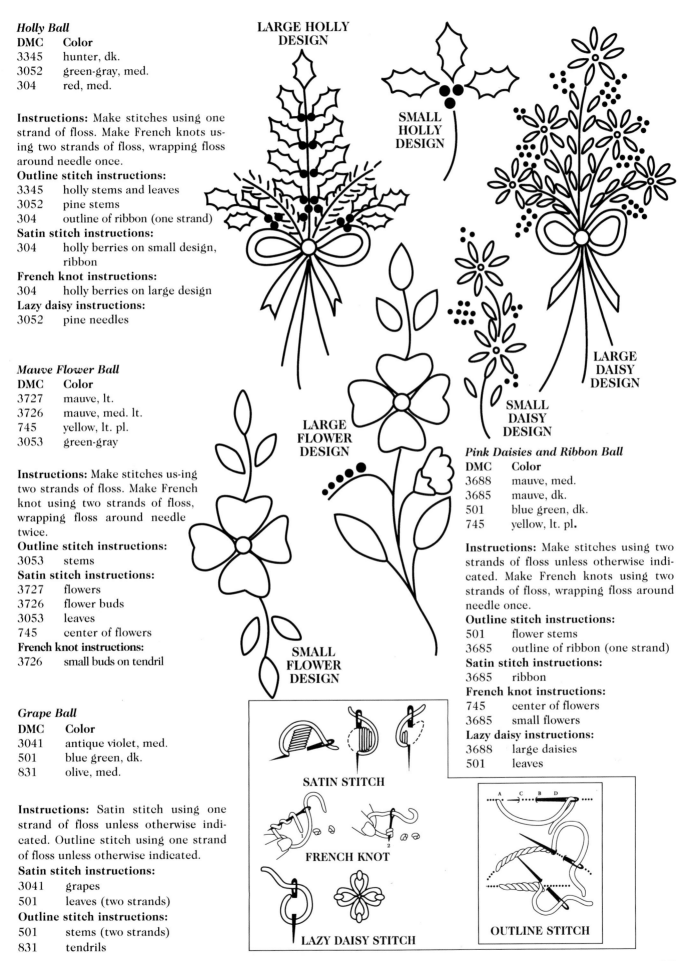

LARGE HOLLY DESIGN

SMALL HOLLY DESIGN

LARGE FLOWER DESIGN

SMALL FLOWER DESIGN

SMALL DAISY DESIGN

LARGE DAISY DESIGN

Pink Daisies and Ribbon Ball

DMC	Color
3688	mauve, med.
3685	mauve, dk.
501	blue green, dk.
745	yellow, lt. pl.

Instructions: Make stitches using two strands of floss unless otherwise indicated. Make French knots using two strands of floss, wrapping floss around needle once.

Outline stitch instructions:

501	flower stems
3685	outline of ribbon (one strand)

Satin stitch instructions:

3685	ribbon

French knot instructions:

745	center of flowers
3685	small flowers

Lazy daisy instructions:

3688	large daisies
501	leaves

SATIN STITCH

FRENCH KNOT

LAZY DAISY STITCH

OUTLINE STITCH

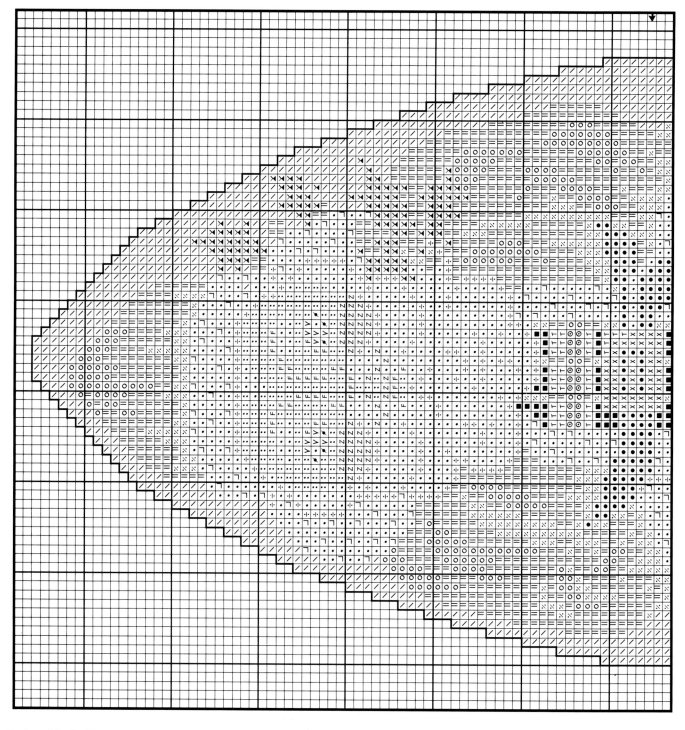

Saint Nick Tree Topper

Materials:
16 " x 11 " piece 14-count cross stitch fabric
11¾" x 6⅓" scrap complementary fabric
   (for backing)
11¾" x 6⅓" scrap medium-weight interfacing
Green thread
Hand-sewing needle
Scissors
Straight pins
Measuring tape
Iron
Sewing machine (optional)

Note: Materials listed will make one *Saint Nick Tree Topper.*

1. Complete cross stitch following instructions given.
2. Place interfacing on back side of cross-stitch fabric and pin. Sew pieces together, following perimeter of stitched design, to form a single front piece with which to work. Remove pins.
3. Place assembled, stitched front and backing pieces with right sides together and pin. Sew pieces together following perimeter of stitched design. Remove pins. Trim seams.

Overcast or zigzag raw edges to prevent fraying.
4. Sew a narrow hem in bottom raw edges of fabric to prevent fraying. Press.
5. Turn excess fabric at bottom of tree topper to inside of tree topper, using bottom edge of stitched design as a guide for turning. Press. Whipstitch hemmed edges of fabric in place, catching only the interfacing on front side. Turn tree topper right-side out. Press.

Note: Outline around design is a guideline for finishing and is not to be backstitched.

Shaded portion indicates overlap from previous page.

Symbol	DMC	Color
⁒	498	red, dk.
‖	321	red
o	335	rose
●	310	black
÷	415	pearl gray
·	white	white
F	353	peach flesh
:	948	peach flesh, vy. lt.
Z	224	pink, lt.
∧	838	beige-brown, vy. dk.
⌐	840	beige-brown, med.
Y	842	beige-brown, vy. lt.
−	433	brown, med.
L	435	brown, vy. lt.
⌀	939	navy, vy. dk.
=	824	blue, vy. dk.
S	825	blue, dk.
V	813	blue, lt.
♥	827	blue, vy. lt.
≠	909	emerald, vy. dk.
■	911	emerald, med.
T	913	Nile green, med.
⊙	955	Nile green, lt.
⊥	783	gold
X	725	topaz
+	726	topaz, lt.
✗	469	avocado
\	895	green, dk.

Fabric: 14-count white Aida from Zweigart®
Stitch count: 141H x 73W
Design size:

11-count	12⅞" x 6⅝"
14-count	10⅛" x 5¼"
18-count	7⅞" x 4"
22-count	6⅓" x 3"

Instructions: Cross stitch using two strands of floss.

37

HOLIDAY GIFTS

This is the season for whispers, hidden packages, late-night stitching, and last-minute wrapping! Even though you always finish just in the nick of time, thoughts of holiday gift-giving start months earlier—especially for those with busy hands who craft or stitch presents every year. Making gifts requires careful planning of time and energies. The ideas gathered will bring great satisfaction to you, the maker; and they are sure to bring smiles to those who receive these gifts of the heart.

You'll find both challenging and easily accomplished projects in the following pages. The Elegant Pillows, stitched on velvet, will take some time and will be treasured for years to come. In contrast, the stuffed Christmas Rabbit and Bear can be made from any fabric and in a short amount of time. Is there a little girl in your life that needs a new doll to love? The Christmas Peasant Doll, made from yarns and fabrics, will be welcomed with open arms. Make one for yourself and use her as a lovely decoration. Select fabric scraps that will remind you of well-liked sewing projects and create a custom-dressed doll.

Look over these great gift suggestions, select your favorites, and begin your crafting and sewing with those that will take the most time for completion. Many of the projects will require an investment of time, while others were chosen for the "last minute" person who performs best under pressure. The important thing is to make a list and get started early. Set a goal for finishing your gifts and stick to it. Your last few days before Christmas can then be spent leisurely wrapping gifts and anticipating the delight your handiwork will bring to others.

Sewing

For the crafter, Christmas is a time when "seaming" talents shine. In addition to holiday garments, toys and collectibles are made from a secret stash of material that has been tucked away for years. Most crafters have a collection of fabric scraps, lace bits, and yarn pieces saved for the day when a potential use might surface. Many times, scraps saved from room decorating projects are perfect for use in sewing projects that will accent the room's decor.

The *Christmas Peasant Doll* is one of the cutest craft creations for the approaching holiday season. Completed using basic sewing techniques, she's dressed in clothing made from several complementary holiday prints. With her embroidered facial features and her yarn braids, she may remind you of the dolls you played with at Grandma's house when you were young. Use this doll as a focal point for tabletop yuletide decorating or craft her to give to a special little girl when she comes visiting during the holidays.

This fabric duo at right makes a seasonal appearance and stays for the rest of the year. One look at these winsome little fellows, and you just have to have them for decorating as well as for giving! The elegant look of taffeta and sparkle satin makes these stuffed loveables suitable for use in traditional decorating. Craft them in colorful Christmas calicos or try a fuzzy, warm, plaid flannel; and they will be perfect for seasonal decorating with a touch of country simplicity. You can go from posh to traditional in the blink of an eye; and when you're finished, you'll have a pair of festive cuddlers youngsters of all ages will enjoy.

Left—*Make the* Christmas Peasant Doll's *braids to match your daughter's hair and customize the doll's dress to match your child's room.*

Above—*These cute animals make precious baby gifts when sewed in soft pastel fabrics or terry cloth. You should omit the ribbons and bows for baby's safety. Select a filling that is washable, and toddlers can take their stuffed friends with them anywhere. Just wash and dry, and they'll be ready to go again!*

Holly and mistletoe have long been the greenery of choice for many festive occasions. Traditionally mistletoe is hung from doorways. Everyone dreams of being caught under the mistletoe by his or her special someone for a magical Christmas Eve kiss.

Holly, a deep rich-green plant, is known for its lovely red berries and crisp wax-like leaves that make a wonderful addition to wreaths and yulelog arrangements. The tribute to holly is found in many holiday songs and carols that are sung throughout the season.

For the stitcher with advanced needle skills, these two seasonal favorites, holly and mistletoe, have found their way into holiday gift giving. Throw pillows add a festive touch to any chair or couch, and this pair will be used every year with great pride. Traditional appliqué, worked on velveteen and combined with rattail cord, embroidery floss, and pearl beads, gives these pieces a sumptuous look for more formal decorating. Although the velveteen makes these projects a bit more challenging to complete than projects created with less tricky fabric, their timeless, lasting beauty will be well worth the extra dollars and effort. The many beautiful trims and cording available at fabric stores offer a variety of finishing options. Many braids and cordings have more than one color twisted together. Find a special one for your fine work, or make your own following our easy instructions.

Right—When finishing your pillow, make sure the cover is the same size as the pillow form. This will give your work a professional look.

Left and above—Using the same pattern pieces, the traditional trio can be made as a wall hanging or a free-standing decoration.

A favorite part of the traditional Christmas story is the account of the three wise men. These elegant magi, re-created on padded, tea-cozy-style covers and shown resting on the hearth, remind us of the real reason we celebrate Christmas. Rich fabrics and machine-appliqué techniques are used to craft these large-scale quilted designs before slipping them over plastic two-liter bottles filled with sand. For safety reasons, place them far enough away from the flames so that the plastic bottles do not melt or lose their shape.

Mantels and the area over the fireplace provide a lovely display area for your handwork. Much attention is given to decorating this area during the holidays as thoughts turn to cozy nights shared with family sitting around the fire.

Wall hangings are very popular decorating items and look wonderful hung above the fireplace. Using the same pattern pieces and sewing techniques, you can make this companion wall hanging to complement *The Magi* trio. The lucky person on your gift list will have decorations that will be cherished for years to come.

Experiment with fabric colors when making these designs. Never shy away from a sewing project if the colors shown do not match your decor. You be the designer and mix and match fabric colors and patterns to achieve the look you want. You will be amazed how much fun it is to customize colors and fabrics to suit your own needs.

Cross Stitch

If you are looking for an unusual gift for your favorite stitching buddy, this quick-to-stitch pillow is your answer. Did your mother spend many hours teaching you how to stitch? Make this pillow as a wonderful tribute to the countless times she rethreaded your needle or helped you carefully rip out your not-so-perfect stitches.

Designed with the needleart enthusiast in mind, this unique organizer is both practical and decorative. Stitched on fourteen-count Aida cloth, the simple cross-stitch pattern is easy to assemble and practical, yet pretty, to use. The loop at the lower left-hand corner serves as a hanger for a floss ring, and the grosgrain ribbon keeps scissors ready at hand. The pocket on the back stores everything from pens to seam rippers to small charts, and the pillow itself serves as a giant pincushion. The verse is appropriate for stitchers everywhere; and when personalized with initials and a date, this pretty pillow makes a wonderful gift for a friend!

If you are looking for a great gift for the granddaughter you taught to cross stitch, make this for her and stitch both of your names instead of the verse on the pillow. Purchase a gold needle and a fine pair of scissors and present the entire ensemble to her for a treasured keepsake. Or attach a pair of your own scissors. She will love having Grandma's things to stitch with.

Decorating for Christmas gives us the opportunity to gather our family and share in the delights of adding festive touches all over our house. One of the traditional decorations is the French horn, embellished with touches of greenery and a big bow. The

Right—A gold frame enhances the metallic embroidery thread used to create this elegant piece. Select a frame deep enough to allow space for the beads.

Left—Easy stitching and finishing make this a sure-to-please gift for the holidays. The large pocket and attachments hold all of your stitching needs in a very attractive pillow to place by your favorite stitching chair.

French horn is the lead instrument in *The Nutcracker Suite,* and the sounds of this refined instrument are associated with this enchanting holiday ballet as its clear melodic tone is heard over the shuffling of feet in the "March of the Toy Soldiers." The elegant cross-stitch design, with sparkling metallic thread and extra-large glass beads, is a great interpretation of that instrument and is perfect for giving a touch of Christmas glitter to a tabletop. Given as a gift, this piece will be enjoyed for years and will be a reminder of the thoughtfulness of the stitcher.

Crochet

There is nothing more appreciated than handmade gifts that can be used year-round. Crochet, a simple hook-and-thread technique, continues to be one of the most popular forms of needlework. Treasured through the years, the work that was done years ago becomes more beautiful with time and is relatively easy to care for. Beautiful crocheted edging, when attached to a set of towels for the powder room, will make a wonderful gift, especially when color coordinated to match the room.

Above—The lovely pointed edging, shown in three sizes, has a delicate appearance and looks beautiful whipstitched to the lower edge of the linens.

Crochet is quite durable and will probably out-last the towel. When the towel becomes worn, the edging can be removed and attached to a new towel and enjoyed for years to come.

For an extraspecial someone, include crocheted sachet bags tied with colorful ribbon. Fill the bag with a fragrant potpourri or the traditional lavender for use in a linen closet. The small crocheted bags hold cedar chips nicely and can be placed in storage bags with your fine wool sweaters during the summer months. If you prefer to display your fine handwork, hang these sachet bags on the bedpost during the holidays, filled with spruce potpourri, to add a touch of holiday fragrance to your bedroom.

Above—These edgings need to be used on dark-colored towels so that the design shows clearly. If you choose lighter colored linens, you may want to substitute a dark crochet thread for making the edgings in order to create a sharp contrast.

Crafting

When friends compliment you on the lovely fragrance of your home, share your secret and present them with a pomander to take home. An orange, lemon, or lime covered with decoratively placed whole cloves makes a simple but welcome gift that will last for the holidays.

Many hostesses choose to use the decorated fruit in their centerpieces and embellish each with holiday ribbon and fresh leaves pinned in place. The aroma is still delightful, and the fruit is very colorful in arrangements. For a festive touch, mix oranges, limes, lemons, grapefruits, and small kumquats in one large bowl with fresh evergreens and nuts.

Below—Gather your family members and see who can make the most interesting pomander for the breakfast room table centerpiece. Children love this safe and fun way of helping Mom with the decorating.

'Twas the Night Before Christmas has always been a favorite story of young and old alike. Every child has visions of Santa parking his sleigh and his eight tiny reindeer on the steep roof and then proceeding to leave presents under the tree inside the house. Imaginations run wild as you hear the sleigh bells approaching from a distance, or at least you think you hear them! This smaller version of Santa's sleigh will be perfect for holiday decorating. Chances are it will bring to mind fond childhood memories for all who see it during this joyous season.

For a different twist to decorating, put small wrapped presents in the sleigh and set it under the tree. You might choose to display prized ornaments in the sleigh seat and use the sleigh as a centerpiece. It makes a wonderful container for candy canes and special holiday candy. If you have a collection of Santas, gather them around this crimson chariot and place your cherished one inside. This is a versatile decoration and will be fun to give or to keep.

Right, above, and left—
Off-white trim adds a
decorative touch to the
sleigh. Glue holiday
greenery to the sides,
as shown, or attach an
assortment of small bells
with ribbons.

This lovable trio of magazine carolers is made using a variation of the pass-the-day craft that we all learned in grammar school. Thinking back on the fun inspired the creation of these precious harmonizers, using some modern-day painting techniques and supplies. Music lovers will enjoy adding these decorations to their collection, and you'll have the fun of making these winsome heralds. The materials needed to complete this paper choir are commonly available at craft stores or stored away in your scrap basket. Children enjoy these and can assist in folding the magazine pages. An ingenious room mother could assist in the classroom and have each child make one of his or her own to display in the classroom and then take home after Christmas.

Below—Save your magazines and enjoy this as the ultimate recycling project for Christmas!

Christmas Peasant Doll

Materials:

½ yd. 44/45"-wide unbleached muslin

½ yd. 44/45"-wide red print fabric

10"-square piece green print fabric (for kerchief)

8"-square piece white border-print fabric (for apron)

8"-square piece green felt (for boots)

6–8 oz. polyester filling

½ yd. ¼"-wide white satin ribbon

1 yd. ¼"-wide red satin ribbon with gold edging

1 small gold bell

1 skein Coats & Clark Red Heart Worsted Weight yarn, color: yellow

1 spool **each** Coats Dual Duty Plus thread, colors: 256 Natural, 01 White, 177 Kerry Green, 128 Red, 157-A Yellow

1 skein **each** J. & P. Coats 6-strand embroidery floss, colors: 6226 (green), 3000 (red), 3281 (light pink)

Tailor's chalk or pencil

Small amount blush   Straight pins

Pinking shears   Scissors

Hand-sewing needle   Iron

Sewing machine (optional)

Note: Please read all instructions carefully before beginning, making special note of seam allowances.

1. Enlarge pattern pieces as indicated. Cut out.

2. Fold muslin in half and trace half-body shape on fold of muslin twice, arm shape twice, and leg shape twice. **DO NOT CUT OUT.** Stitch around marked lines of arm shapes and leg shapes, using natural thread and leaving openings for turning in top of each leg shape and shoulder end of each arm shape. Cut out arm and leg shapes, using pinking shears and trimming to within ⅛" of stitching. Cut out half-body shapes, using pinking shears and trimming to within ⅛" of marked lines. Unfold shapes and pin together, aligning marked lines, and stitch along marked lines, using natural thread and leaving an opening for turning in bottom of body. Clip corners and curves on arm, leg, and body shapes. Turn each piece right-side out and stuff firmly with polyester filling. Slip stitch openings closed. Sew arms and legs to body.

3. Mark facial features on doll, referring to photo on page 40 for placement. Apply blush to cheeks. Embroider mouth, using six strands red floss. (**Note:** Mouth is a V-shape made with a straight stitch that is couched down in the center.) Embroider eyes, using six strands green floss. (**Note:** Embroider each eye by beginning in center and making straight stitch for each "spoke" of eye, referring to photo.) Make French knot for nose, using six strands pink floss and wrapping floss around needle once.

4. Fold felt in half. Trace two boot shapes onto felt with tailor's chalk or pencil. Stitch around boot shapes, using green thread, following traced outlines, and leaving tops of boots unstitched. Cut out boots close to stitching and along traced outline at top. Turn boots right-side out and slip onto doll's feet.

5. Cut an 18" x 10" rectangle from red print fabric for bodice. Fold into quarters by folding in half twice. Trace bodice shape onto folded rectangle, aligning short fold side of pattern and long fold side of pattern with corresponding folds of fabric. Cut out fabric ¼" away from marked lines. Press open. Fold bodice fabric in half along lengthwise edge with right sides together. Stitch sleeve, underarm, and side seams in one continuous motion, using red thread. Clip curves. Turn right-side out. Clip where indicated by dotted lines on pattern, making an opening in neck area in an H-shape. Slip bodice onto doll. Turn raw edges under ¼" on sleeves and gather with red thread to fit wrists tightly. Turn raw edges under ¼" along neck edges. Pinch fabric at shoulders, covering any raw edges and making shoulders of bodice slightly puffy. Tack in place using red thread.

6. Cut two 10" square pieces from red print fabric for skirt. Place squares with right sides together. Sew along opposite sides, using a ¼" seam allowance and forming a tube. Narrowly hem one raw-edge end of tube. Hem all edges of apron square except top, using white thread. Center apron on center front of skirt and baste apron to skirt. Turn raw edge of skirt under ½" to inside. Stitch close to raw edge to form casing. On right side of back of skirt, make small slit in casing. Thread

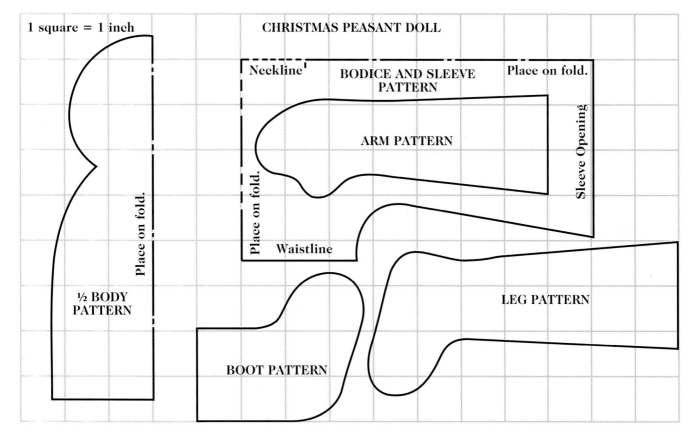

1 square = 1 inch

CHRISTMAS PEASANT DOLL

½ BODY PATTERN

Place on fold.

Neckline

BODICE AND SLEEVE PATTERN

Place on fold.

ARM PATTERN

Waistline

Place on fold.

Sleeve Opening

LEG PATTERN

BOOT PATTERN

white ribbon through casing, draw up ribbon to gather skirt slightly, and slip skirt onto doll. Continue to draw up ribbon to make skirt fit doll's waist snugly. Tie to secure.

7. Cut red ribbon into three equal lengths. Set aside.

8. Wrap yarn around four fingers several times. Remove from fingers and tack at top of doll's head, centering approximately ¼" back from seam and placing so that loops go from back to front, not from side to side. Trim loop ends at front of doll's head to make bangs. Cut twenty-four 30" lengths of yarn for braids and group together. Center yarn atop head. Backstitch over yarn to make a part, using yellow thread. Separate yarn on one side of head into three sections of eight strands each and braid to within 1" from end of yarn. Tie length of red ribbon at end of braid to secure and tie bow in ribbon. Repeat for second braid on other side of doll's head.

9. Fold 10" square piece green print fabric in half diagonally to make a triangle, placing right sides together. Stitch along open edges of triangle ¼" in from raw edges, leaving a 1" opening along one side for turning. Turn right-side out and slip stitch opening closed. Place kerchief around doll's head and overlap ends under doll's chin. Tack ends together at overlap and tack to bodice to secure.

10. Run remaining red ribbon through bell. Tie ribbon in bow and tack to doll's hand, using natural thread.

Christmas Rabbit and Bear

Note: For these projects, a general list of materials has been given. Specific materials for each project have been listed separately.

General materials:
Tracing paper **and** pencil
Disappearing-ink fabric-marking pen
Polyester filling   Hand-sewing needle
White thread   Scissors
Crochet hook **or** similar object (for turning small areas)
Sewing machine with zipper foot
Hot glue gun

Materials for *Christmas Rabbit*:
½ yd. 44/45"-wide teal sparkle satin
Thread to match
12" length 1½"-wide white flat lace
⅞ yd. ⅛"-wide pink satin ribbon
⅞ yd. ⅛"-wide burgundy satin ribbon
⅞ yd. ⅜"-wide burgundy satin ribbon
1 pink rosette (available in fabric/craft stores)

Materials for *Christmas Bear*:
½ yd. 44/45"-wide coral moiré taffeta
Thread to match

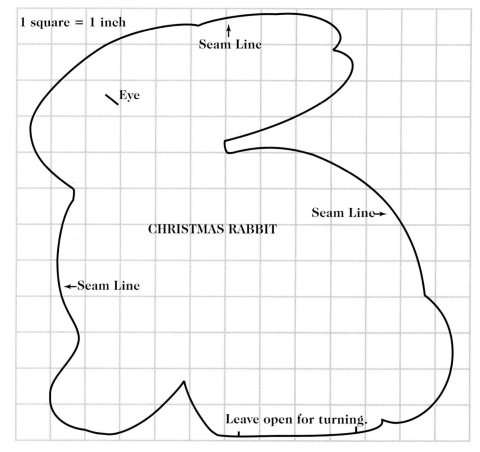

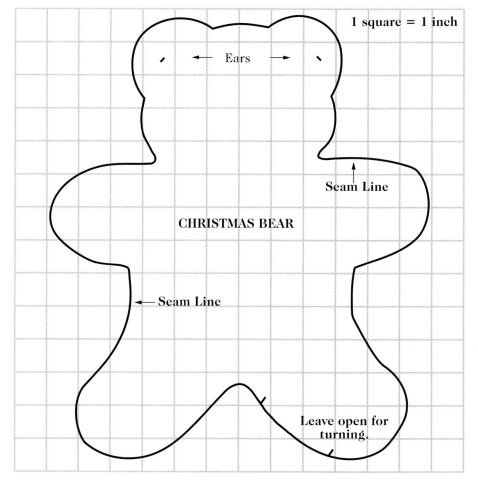

12" length 1"-wide white flat lace
1 yd. ⅛"-wide white satin ribbon
1 yd. ⅛"-wide green satin ribbon
1 yd. ⅛"-wide red satin ribbon
Small wooden heart (optional, available in
  craft stores)

Note: Materials listed will make one *Christmas Rabbit* and one *Christmas Bear*.

1. Enlarge rabbit and bear patterns as indicated. Place a piece of tracing paper over each pattern and trace, marking openings for turning and all placement symbols as indicated. Cut out traced patterns. Cut two squares of fabric for each animal, making each square 1" larger on all sides than widest and tallest points of pattern. Trace around rabbit pattern on wrong side of one piece of teal sparkle satin and around bear pattern on wrong side of one piece of coral taffeta, using disappearing-ink fabric-marking pen and marking openings for turning. **DO NOT CUT OUT SHAPES.**

2. Attach zipper foot to sewing machine. Place like fabric pieces with right sides together and sew along pen lines, leaving openings for turning as indicated. Cut out shapes, leaving ¼" seam allowance. Clip seam allowance at curves and corners and turn shapes right-side out. Use rounded end of crochet hook to completely turn ears and other small areas. Refer to patterns and use disappearing-ink fabric-marking pen to lightly mark placement of features. Stuff shapes with polyester filling. Use rounded end of crochet hook to stuff small amounts of filling into small areas. **DO NOT OVERSTUFF.** Whipstitch opening closed.

3. Run a gathering thread through each length of lace along edge, gather, and overlap short ends to form a circle. Tack at overlap to secure.

4. Glue lace circle on bear at left chest area to mark heart placement. Hand draw a small heart, approximately 1" wide and 1" tall, and cut two heart shapes from taffeta scraps. Place right sides together and sew by hand, using ¼" seam allowance and leaving an opening for turning. Clip curves and corners and turn right-side out. Stuff with polyester filling. Whipstitch opening closed.

Option: You may substitute a purchased wooden heart. Glue heart in center of lace, referring to photo on page 41 for placement.

5. Thread needle with doubled thread and knot thread ends. To make eye, insert needle through rabbit where eye is indicated, working from back side of animal. Pull thread through. Insert needle again, this time from the front, approximately ¼" away from first insertion. Pull thread tightly and repeat. Secure thread on back side of rabbit and clip thread tails. Repeat for bear to make ears where ears are indicated.

6. Tie ribbons in knot around rabbit's neck and pull ribbons through center of lace circle. Tie ribbons in bow to secure. Tie ribbons in knot around bear's neck and then in bow atop knot.

7. Tie knots randomly in bow streamers on both rabbit and bear.

8. Glue rosette to middle of bow at rabbit's neck.

Pomanders

Materials:
Oranges (**Note:** Purchase number desired.)
Cloves (approximately 120 for **each** orange)
16" length ⅜"-wide green satin ribbon for **each** orange or 1½ yds. ⅜"-wide green satin ribbon for **each** orange (**Note:** 16" length will make bows shown on oranges grouped in bowl. A 1½-yds. length will make bow shown on orange displayed in gift box. Refer to photo on page 49.)
Awl, ice pick, **or** fork
Long straight pins

Note: Pomanders are perishable and should be made close to time of use. Lemons or limes can also be used to make pomanders. Remember to recalculate the number of cloves needed.

1. Hold each orange so that stem area is at top. Punch holes in oranges, using awl, ice pick, or single tine of fork, leaving enough space between holes to accommodate heads of cloves and referring to photo on page 49 for hole placement. Punch holes in rows radiating out from stem area of each orange.

2. Insert one clove into each hole.

3. Tie lengths of green satin ribbon into bows or multiple-loop bows and pin one ribbon bow at top center of each orange, referring to photo for placement.

Elegant Pillows

Materials:
1 yd. 44/45"-wide ivory cotton velveteen fabric
½ yd. 44/45"-wide lightweight green cotton velveteen fabric
½ yd. 44/45"-wide lightweight green lining fabric (taffeta **or** cotton)
1½ yds. green rattail cord (for stems on mistletoe pillow)
1½ yds. brown rattail cord (for stems on holly pillow)
Thread to match velveteen fabrics and cord
1 skein each #5 pearl cotton, colors: green, brown (for small stems)
1 skein red #5 pearl cotton (for holly berries)
Twelve 5mm off-white pearl beads (for mistletoe)

4 yds. purchased cording and 8 tassels **or** 50 yds. **each** ivory Persian wool and gold yarn
Two 16" square pillow forms
Very fine pins
Fine hand-sewing needle
Beading **or** embroidery needle
Scissors
Disappearing-ink fabric-marking pen
Cardboard (for templates)
Stapler and staples
Sewing machine
Eleven 10mm red sequins (optional, for holly berries)

Finished size of each pillow: 16" x 16"
Note: Leaves are lined, making smooth curves and finished, neat edges that are easy to appliqué. Appliqué can be done the traditional way by adding ¼" seam allowances to leaves and turning edges under as you blind stitch leaves in place.

1. Enlarge patterns as indicated. Make cardboard templates of large leaf and small leaf for each pillow. Trace around leaf shapes on wrong side of green lining fabric, leaving approximately ½" between shapes. For mistletoe pillow, trace ten large and eight small leaves. For holly pillow, trace seven large and seven small leaves. Pin lining and velveteen with right sides together, being careful to keep pins to outside of leaf shapes, as they may leave permanent marks in velveteen. With machine stitch length set to 18–20 stitches per inch, sew around all leaf shapes along traced lines, leaving open to turn as indicated. Cut out leaves, leaving a ⅛" seam allowance. Clip concave curves and turn right-side out.

2. Cut two 17" squares from ivory velveteen for each pillow. Referring to pattern, place leaves on right side of one square of ivory velveteen, pinning from wrong side of pillow top into leaf lining only, so as not to mark top surface of velveteen with pins. Trace stem lines onto pillow top, using disappearing-ink fabric-marking pen.
Note: Marker will disappear in time; so if you do not plan to complete these projects now, you may wish to baste in stem lines, using a long running stitch.

3. Sew cord down on marked stem lines. Running stitches approximately ⅛" long, worked with matching thread, will blend into the cord.

4. Appliqué leaves in place, using invisible stitches and tucking rattail stem ends under leaves.

5. Outline stitch small stems, using pearl cotton to match large stems and referring to Illustration 1.

6. To make holly berries, tack 10mm red sequin in place for each berry. Use red #5 pearl cotton and stitch over sequins as shown in Illustration 2.

Note: Sequins are optional but provide perfect circle patterns over which to stitch.

7. To make mistletoe berries, use a beading needle and off-white thread to attach pearl beads as indicated on pattern.

8. Assemble each pillow by sewing front and back squares together with right sides of fabric together, using ½" seam allowance and leaving bottom of pillow open for turning. Trim, turn right-side out, insert pillow form, and blind stitch opening closed.

9. Sew on purchased cording and tassels or make your own to match pillows perfectly.

10. To make cording, mix ivory Persian wool with gold yarn. Make twisted cord for one edge of pillow at a time. Cut five 1-yard lengths of gold and ivory yarn. Overlapping the two colors approximately ¾", staple the two colors together to form one long length. (Refer to Illustration 3.) Grasp one end of length and hold it tightly while twisting opposite end. When entire length is twisted, bring ends together, holding securely and dividing in middle with one finger. Remove finger from middle. Yarn will twist. When yarn stops twisting, run hand over length several times to smooth and tie loose knot in end opposite staple to hold twist. Center length of twisted cord on pillow edge and hand sew in place from corner to corner, referring to Illustration 4. When all sides are corded, make tassels.

11. To make each tassel, cut ten 8" lengths **each** of gold and ivory yarn. Mix together and place lengths at each corner. Tie at each corner, securing twisted cord and center of 8" lengths. (Refer to Illustration 5.) Remove staples from twisted cord. Untwist excess twisted cord and fluff. (Refer to Illustration 6.) Trim ends to an even length and tie all together approximately ¾" below first tie.

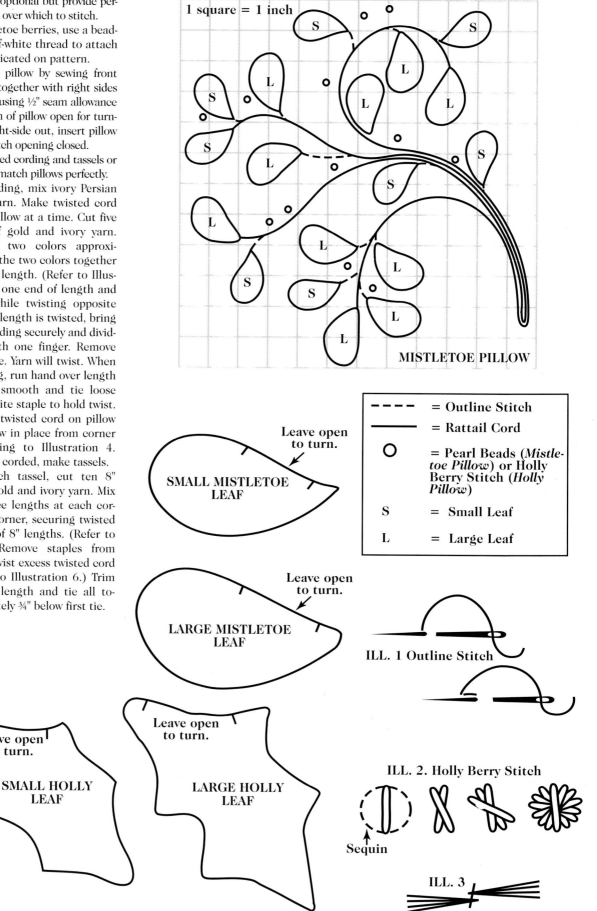

1 square = 1 inch

MISTLETOE PILLOW

SMALL MISTLETOE LEAF — Leave open to turn.

LARGE MISTLETOE LEAF — Leave open to turn.

SMALL HOLLY LEAF — Leave open to turn.

LARGE HOLLY LEAF — Leave open to turn.

- - - - = Outline Stitch

——— = Rattail Cord

○ = Pearl Beads (*Mistletoe Pillow*) or Holly Berry Stitch (*Holly Pillow*)

S = Small Leaf

L = Large Leaf

ILL. 1 Outline Stitch

ILL. 2. Holly Berry Stitch

Sequin

ILL. 3

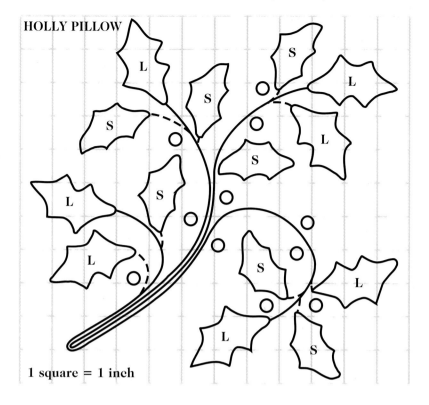

HOLLY PILLOW

1 square = 1 inch

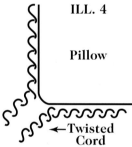

ILL. 4

Pillow

← Twisted Cord

8" lengths of gold and ivory—added to make tassel plumper.

ILL. 5

Tie here first.

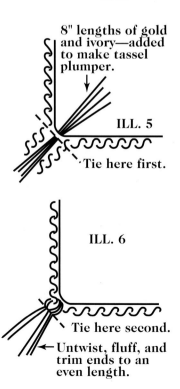

ILL. 6

Tie here second.

← Untwist, fluff, and trim ends to an even length.

The Magi

Note: Please read instructions carefully before beginning. Finished projects show wise men facing right. Note that on paper patterns, they face left. This is correct, and all patterns should be used right-side up, as process used for fusing with Wonder-Under® will reverse fabric designs from the way they appear on paper patterns.

Wise Men for a Mantel

Materials:

2 yds. osnaburg or other heavy-weight coarse cotton cloth, prewashed and ironed

Scraps of calico with Oriental look, chintz, linen, felt, suede, etc., prewashed and ironed

Thread to match osnaburg and fabric scraps

2 yds. thin batting

2 yds. Pellon® Wonder-Under® Transfer Web

3 yds. medium cord, plain **or** prefinished

Fabric for bias cording strips (if making cording)

2 yds. Pellon® Decor-bond™ #809 heavy iron-on interfacing

Colored pencils **or** permanent fine markers to match men's hair

3 plastic 2-liter bottles

Sand **or** aquarium gravel (for weighting bottles)

Sewing machine with zigzag stitch and zipper foot

Iron and press cloth

1. Enlarge pattern pieces as indicated. Trace all pattern pieces except background shape onto paper side of Wonder-Under®, labeling pieces as you go. Broken lines are cutting lines indicating where one piece lies under another.

2. Following manufacturer's instructions for fusing, fuse traced pattern pieces to wrong side of fabric. Cut out. **Note:** No seam allowance is needed for machine appliqué.

3. To prepare backing, cut two **EACH** of background shape from osnaburg, batting, and interfacing for **EACH** wise man.

4. Arrange cut wise men shapes on osnaburg, referring to pattern and leaving 1½" at bottom of background shape. Fuse. Pin osnaburg to one layer of thin batting. Baste if desired. Using thread to match individual colors, satin stitch edges of wise men, omitting faces, hands, and beards. [**Note:** Machine satin stitch (tight zigzag) should be less than ⅛" wide.] Clip all threads. Remove pins. Fuse heavy interfacing to back of thin batting, following manufacturer's instructions for fusing. Draw in eyes and brows with colored pencils or markers.

5. To determine width to cut bias fabric strips for covering cording, fold one corner of fabric over cord and pin close to cord. Measure out ⅝" from pin and mark. Remove fabric from cord. Cut out strip along bias of fabric. (**Note:** Measured strip will become pattern.) Cut bias strips and sew together, using ¼" seam allowance, to form 3-yd.-long cording strip.

6. To make cording, stitch one end of cord to one end of cording strip, placing cord on wrong side of strip and centering. Fold cording strip around cord, placing wrong sides of fabric together and aligning raw edges. Pin as needed to get started. Place cording under zipper foot with raw edges to right. Machine stitch close to cord, being careful not to crowd cord.

7. Pin cording around background shape, placing cording atop right side of fabric with raw edge of cording toward raw edge of fabric and aligning stitching line on cording with seam line on background shape. (**Note:** Do not place cording across bottom of shape.) Machine sew cording to background shape, using zipper foot and following stitching line on cording as a guide. Remove pins.

8. Layer second piece of interfacing, then thin batting, then osnaburg. (**Note:** This will be back side of background shape.) Fuse interfacing, and then sew back to appliquéd front, with right sides of osnaburg together, leaving bottom of shape open. Turn up ½" at bottom and hem by

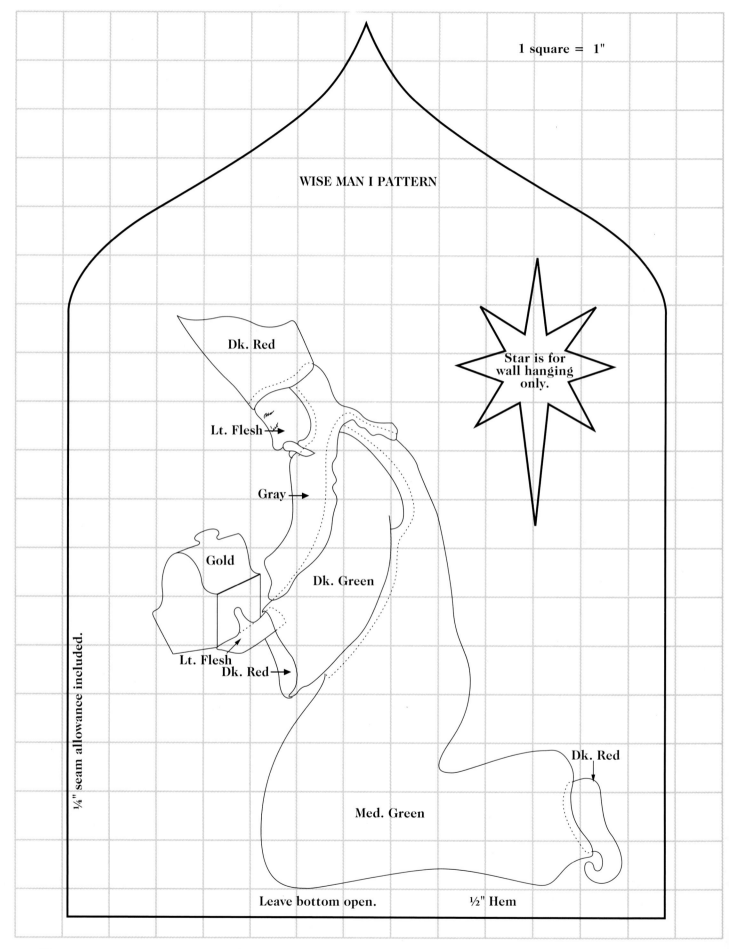

1 square = 1"

WISE MAN I PATTERN

Dk. Red

Star is for
wall hanging
only.

Lt. Flesh

Gray

Gold

Dk. Green

Lt. Flesh

Dk. Red

Dk. Red

Med. Green

¼" seam allowance included.

Leave bottom open.   ½" Hem

hand. Slip finished shapes over plastic two-liter bottles to hold them upright on mantel or table. Fold flat to store.

Note: Fill plastic bottles with sand or aquarium gravel to lend stability.

Wise Men Wall Hanging
Materials:
1 yd. 44/45"-wide unbleached muslin, prewashed and ironed
1 yd. 44/45"-wide backing fabric, prewashed and ironed
Scraps of calico with Oriental look, chintz, linen, felt, suede, etc., prewashed and ironed
Thread to match muslin, backing fabric, and fabric scraps
2 yds. 44/45"-wide thin batting
2 yds. Pellon® Wonder-Under® Transfer Web
4 yds. extra-wide bias binding
Metallic gold quilting thread
6" x 8" scrap gold lamé (for star)
Colored pencils **or** permanent fine markers to match men's hair
Yardstick or dowel (for hanging)
Scissors   Sewing machine

Finished size: 30" x 40"

1. Prepare wise men and star pieces (using gold lamé for star) as for mantel decorations, omitting background shapes. Cut muslin, backing, and two thin batting pieces 31" x 41" **each**. Fuse wise men and star to muslin, referring to photo on page 45 for placement. Place muslin with wise men and star right-side down atop flat surface. Place two layers thin batting and backing with right side up atop muslin. Smooth and pin all layers. Baste. With machine stitch length set for tiny stitches, sew around outer edges of wise men, using thread to match muslin. (**Note:** This straight stitching at edge of appliqué makes it puff and appear to have been done by hand). Sew clothing lines within appliqué designs, using thread to match fabrics.

2. Sew around star. Hand- or machine- quilt lines in sky radiating from star points, using metallic gold quilting thread.

Note: Using long quilting stitches will allow gold to shine more than if short stitches are used.

3. Square up quilt edges and trim to 30" x 40".

4. To make fabric sleeve for hanging, cut leftover backing fabric into 4" x 40"-long strip. Hem ends to 38". Fold in half along lengthwise edge, placing fabric with wrong sides together and aligning raw edges. Pin raw edge along top of wall hanging. Bind quilt. Hand sew bottom of sleeve to backing. Slip dowel or yardstick through sleeve to hang.

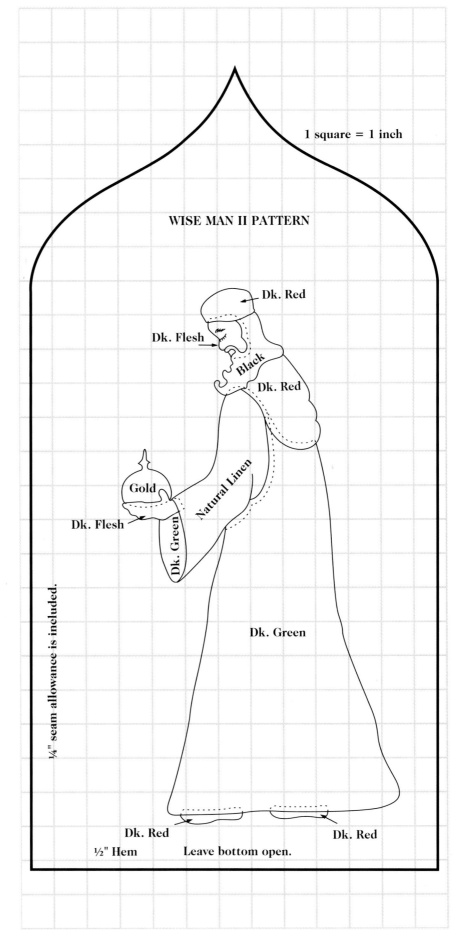

1 square = 1 inch

WISE MAN II PATTERN

Dk. Red

Dk. Flesh

Black

Dk. Red

Gold

Dk. Flesh

Dk. Green

Natural Linen

Dk. Green

¼" seam allowance is included.

Dk. Red

½" Hem   Leave bottom open.   Dk. Red

59

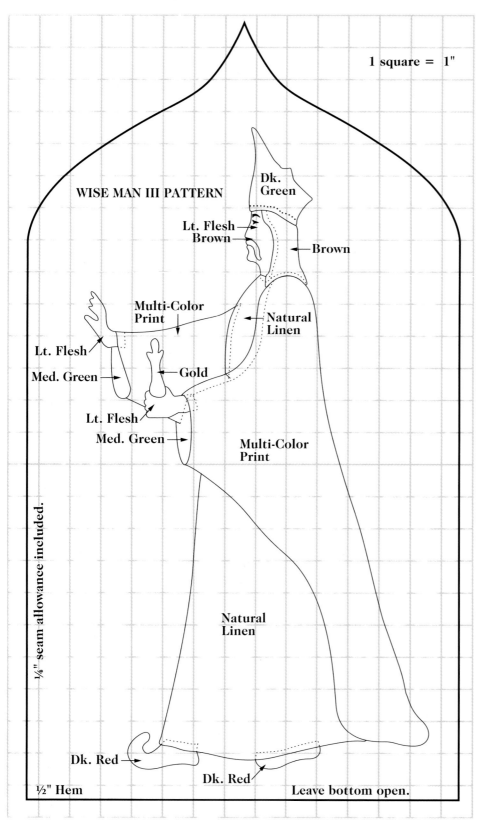

WISE MAN III PATTERN

1 square = 1"

Dk. Green

Lt. Flesh
Brown

Brown

Multi-Color Print

Natural Linen

Lt. Flesh

Med. Green

Gold

Lt. Flesh

Med. Green

Multi-Color Print

Natural Linen

Dk. Red

Dk. Red

¼" seam allowance included.

½" Hem

Leave bottom open.

As Ye Sew Pillow

DMC		Color
Z	904	parrot green, vy. dk.
o	725	topaz
2	349	coral, dk.
●	350	coral, med.
X	640	beige-gray, vy. dk.
bs	318	steel gray, lt.

Fabric: 14-count antique white Aida
Stitch count: 69H x 109W
Design size:

11-count	6⅜" x 10"
14-count	5" x 7¾"
18-count	3¾" x 6⅛"
22-count	3¼" x 5"

Instructions: Cross stitch using two strands of floss. Backstitch using one strand of floss unless indicated otherwise.
Backstitch (bs) instructions:

318	needle (two strands)
904	thread

Materials:
1 yd. 44/45"-wide complementary fabric (for backing, pocket, ruffle, cord, and loop)
Thread to match
2 yds. 2"-wide white eyelet trim (for ruffle)
34" length ⅛"-wide cord
Two ⅜" white buttons
Floss ring
Tapestry needle
½ yd. ⅜"-wide red grosgrain ribbon
Small piece Velcro®
Disappearing-ink fabric-marking pen
Polyester filling
Straight pins
Hand-sewing needle
Scissors
Sewing machine with zipper foot
Iron

Finished size: 10" x 12" on 14-count Aida
Note: Please read all instructions carefully before beginning.

1. Complete cross stitch following instructions given. Attach buttons where indicated on chart by symbol ℬ.
2. Cut fabric pieces as indicated in diagram. Set aside.
3. Cut 2" x 4" fabric scrap to make loop for floss ring. Fold lengthwise with raw edges to center. Press. Fold in half along narrow edge, aligning narrow raw edges, and press. Set aside.
4. To make cording, sew bias strips together to form cording strip, using ¼"

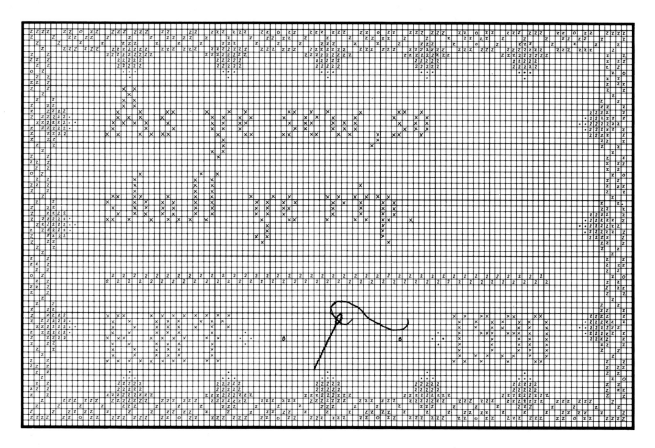

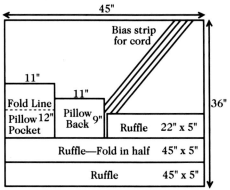

Make Ruffle 110" long x 5" wide.

seam allowance. Stitch one end of cord to one end of cording strip, placing cord on wrong side of strip and centering. Fold cording strip around cord, placing wrong sides of fabric together and aligning raw edges. Pin as needed to get started. Place cording under zipper foot with raw edges to right. Machine stitch close to cord, being careful not to crowd cord.

5. Lightly mark cross-stitch fabric 1" away from stitched border on all sides of design, using disappearing-ink fabric-marking pen. Place cording around perimeter of design with raw edge of cording toward raw edge of cross-stitch fabric, aligning stitching line on cording with pen markings. Machine stitch cording to pillow front, using zipper foot and following stitching line on cording.

Note: Attach grosgrain ribbon and fabric loop for floss ring with cording, referring to photo on page 46 for placement.

6. Machine sew soft, fuzzy side of Velcro® to grosgrain ribbon, placing Velcro® at midpoint between loose end of ribbon and spot where ribbon is attached to pillow front.

7. To make ruffle, sew three fabric ruffle strips together using ½" seam allowances. Press seams open. Fold assembled ruffle strip in half along lengthwise edge with wrong sides together. Press. Pin eyelet trim to assembled ruffle strip, aligning raw edges. Sew pieces together using ½" seam allowance. Remove pins. Run two gathering threads in seam allowance. Pull up threads to gather and pin ruffle to pillow front, using cording as guide for placement and spacing ruffles evenly around perimeter of pillow front. Sew ruffle to pillow front. Remove pins.

8. Fold pillow pocket piece in half along fold line with wrong sides together and topstitch ¼" in from fold. Place on pillow back piece, aligning raw edges along one 11" side. Sew pieces together at sides and bottom.

9. Sew pillow front and back pieces together, placing pieces with right sides of fabric together, using ½" seam allowance, and leaving opening in bottom of pillow for turning. Trim seam allowance and turn pillow right-side out. Stuff

with polyester filling. Whipstitch opening closed.

10. To complete pillow, attach floss ring to loop, stick tapestry needle into pillow front between buttons, and tie scissors to pillow with ribbon.

French Horn

	DMC	Kreinik Metallics	Color
6	319		pistachio, vy. dk.
V	367		pistachio, dk.
II	320		pistachio, med.
▲	780		topaz, vy. dk.
		002HL-BF	gold, high lustre
3	782		topaz, med.
		002HL-BF	gold, high lustre
L	783		gold
		002HL-BF	gold, high lustre
-	725		topaz
		002HL-BF	gold, high lustre
•	814		garnet, dk.
		080HL-BF	garnet, high lustre
M	816		garnet
		080HL-BF	garnet, high lustre
o	347		salmon, dk.
		013-BF	crimson
/	3328		salmon, med.
		013-BF	crimson
✗	321		red
ss	890		pistachio, ul. dk.

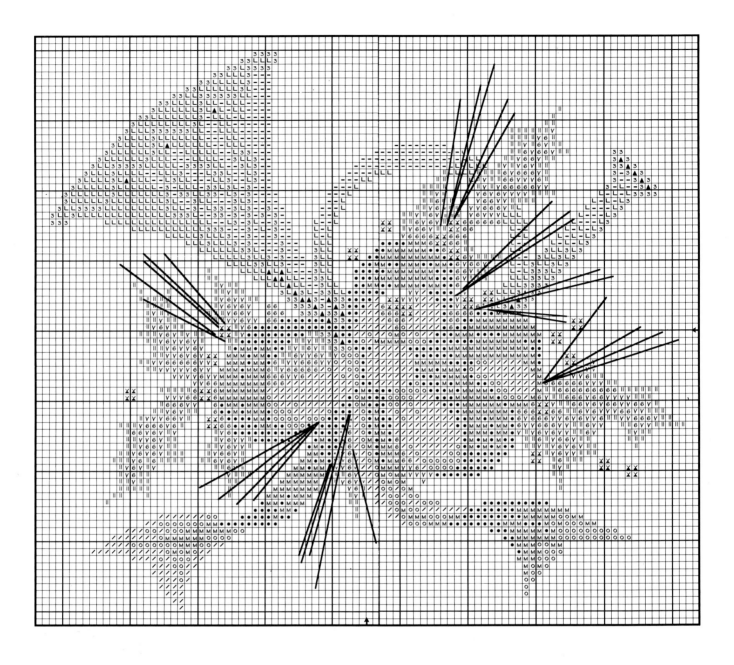

Fabric: 27-count cream linen from Norden Crafts

Stitch count: 80H x 94W

Design size:

14-count	5¾" x 6¾"
18-count	4⅜" x 5¼"
27-count	5⅞" x 7"
32-count	5" x 5⅞"

Instructions: Cross stitch over two threads, using two strands of floss. Make straight stitches (ss) for pine needles, using one strand 890. When DMC and Kreinik Metallics are bracketed together, use one strand DMC and two strands Kreinik Blending Filament.

Option: Use 05025 ruby Mill Hill Glass Pebble Beads where symbol ✕ appears. Use one bead for each berry.

Lacy Potpourri of Peaches

Materials:
400 yds. white size 20 mercerized Crochet Cotton (**Note:** Clark's® Big Ball was used for model.)
Size 9 steel crochet hook **or** size needed to reach gauge of 12 dc = 1"; 11 rows = 2"

Helpful hints: For better tension control, wind thread an extra time around your little or ring finger. Ch 3 at beg of row counts as a dc; on these patterns you may find it easier to go into the ch-3 sp rather than into the third ch at end of row.

To finish and assemble: Cut thread 2" long and weave in ends. Gently wash lace and towels separately. Under damp cloth, lightly press lace to precise shape before hand or machine stitching it to towel.

Uses: Decorate towels, aprons, bed linens, place mats, skirts, and pockets; add spicy *Potpourri Pocket* to dresser drawer or linen shelf, display on bathroom counter, or hang on wall.

Peach Blossoms
Row 1: Ch 27 loosely. Dc in 5th ch from hook, ch 2, sk 2 ch, dc in nxt 16 ch, ch 2, sk 2 ch, dc in nxt 2 ch [= 2 dc, sp, 16 dc, sp, 2 dc].
Row 2: Ch 3 [counts as first dc], turn, dc in nxt dc, ch 2, sk ch-2 sp, dc in nxt 7 dc, ch 2, sk 2 dc, dc in nxt 7 dc, ch 2, sk ch-2 sp, dc in nxt 2 dc [=2 dc, sp, 7 dc, sp, 7 dc, sp, 2 dc].
Row 3: Ch 3, turn, dc in nxt dc, ch 2, dc in nxt 4 dc, ch 5, sc in ch-2 sp, ch 5, sk 3 dc, dc in nxt 4 dc, ch 2, dc in nxt 2 dc [= 2 dc, sp, 4 dc, 2 ch-5 sps, 4 dc, sp, 2 dc].
Row 4: Ch 3, turn, dc in nxt dc, ch 2, dc in nxt 4 dc, 3 dc in sp, ch 2, 3 dc in nxt sp, dc in nxt 4 dc, ch 2, dc in nxt 2 dc [= 2 dc, sp, 7 dc, sp, 7 dc, sp, 2 dc].
Row 5: Ch 3, turn, dc in nxt dc, ch 2, dc in nxt 7 dc, 2 dc in sp, dc in nxt 7 dc, ch 2, dc in nxt 2 dc [= 2 dc, sp, 16 dc, sp, 2 dc].

Row 6: Ch 3, turn, dc in nxt dc, ch 2, dc in nxt 7 dc, ch 2, sk 2 dc, dc in nxt 7 dc, ch 2, dc in nxt 2 dc [= 2 dc, sp, 7 dc, sp, 7 dc, sp, 2 dc].
Row 7: Ch 3, turn, dc in nxt dc, ch 2, dc in nxt 4 dc, ch 5, dc in sp, ch 5, sk 3 dc, dc in nxt 4 dc, ch 2, dc in nxt 2 dc [= 2 dc, sp, 4 dc, 2 ch-5 sps, 4 dc, sp, 2 dc].
Row 8: Ch 3, turn, dc in nxt dc, ch 2, dc in nxt 2 dc, (ch 5, sc in nxt ch-5 sp) 2 times, ch 5, sk 2 dc, dc in nxt 2 dc, ch 2, dc in nxt 2 dc [= 2 dc, sp, 2 dc, 3 ch-5 sps, 2 dc, sp, 2 dc].
Row 9: Ch 3, turn, dc in nxt dc, ch 2, dc in nxt 2 dc, 2 dc in sp, ch 5, sc in center ch-5 sp, ch 5, 2 dc in nxt sp, dc in nxt 2 dc, ch 2, dc in nxt 2 dc [= 2 dc, sp, 4 dc, 2 ch-5 sps, 4 dc, sp, 2 dc].
Row 10: Ch 3, turn, dc in dc, ch 2, dc in nxt 4 dc, 3 dc in sp, ch 2, 3 dc in nxt sp, dc in nxt 4 dc, ch 2, dc in nxt 2 dc [= 2 dc, sp, 7 dc, sp, 7 dc, sp, 2 dc].
Row 11: Ch 3, turn, dc in nxt dc, ch 2, dc in nxt 7 dc, 2 dc in sp, dc in nxt 7 dc, ch 2, dc in nxt 2 dc [= 2 dc, sp, 16 dc, sp, 2 dc].
REPEAT ROWS 2–11 eight times or almost the width of the towel; then make rows 2–5. Fasten off.

Geometric Peach
Row 1: Ch 31 loosely. Dc in 5th ch from hook and nxt 26 ch [= 28 dc].
Row 2: Ch 3 [counts as first dc], turn, dc in nxt 3 dc, (ch 2, sk 2 dc, dc in nxt dc) 2 times, dc in nxt 9 dc, (ch 2, sk 2 dc, dc in nxt dc) 2 times, dc in nxt 3 dc [= 4 dc, 2 sps, 10 dc, 2 sps, 4 dc].
Row 3: Ch 3, turn, dc in nxt 3 dc, 2 dc in sp, dc in nxt dc, ch 2, dc in nxt dc, ch 2, sk 2 dc, dc in nxt 4 dc, ch 2, sk 2 dc, dc in nxt dc, ch 2, dc in nxt dc, 2 dc in sp, dc in nxt 4 dc [= 7 dc, 2 sps, 4 dc, 2 sps, 7 dc].
Row 4: Ch 3, turn, dc in nxt 6 dc, 2 dc in sp, dc in nxt dc, ch 2, dc in nxt dc, ch 2, sk 2 dc, dc in nxt dc, ch 2, dc in nxt dc, 2 dc in sp, dc in nxt 7 dc [= 10 dc, 3 sps, 10 dc].
Row 5: Ch 3, turn, dc in nxt 6 dc, ch 2, sk 2 dc, dc in nxt dc, ch 2, dc in nxt dc, 2 dc in sp, dc in nxt dc, ch 2, dc in nxt dc, ch 2, sk 2 dc, dc in nxt 7 dc [= 7 dc, 2 sps, 4 dc, 2 sps, 7 dc].
Row 6: Ch 3, turn, dc in nxt 3 dc, ch 2, sk 2 dc, dc in nxt dc, ch 2, dc in nxt dc, 2 dc in nxt sp, dc in nxt 4 dc, 2 dc in sp, dc in dc, ch 2, dc in nxt dc, ch 2, sk 2 dc, dc in nxt 4 dc [= 4 dc, 2 sps, 10 dc, 2 sps, 4 dc].
Row 7: Ch 3, turn, dc in nxt 3 dc, (ch 2, dc in nxt dc) 2 times, dc in nxt 9 dc, (ch 2, dc in nxt dc) 2 times, dc in nxt 3 dc [= 4 dc, 2 sps, 10 dc, 2 sps, 4 dc].

REPEAT ROWS 3–7 fifteen times or width of towel, except instead of final row 7 make ch 3, turn, dc in each dc and make 2 dc in each sp [= 28 dc]. Fasten off.

Spice and Peaches in Band and Triangles (shown on peach towels)
Narrow Lace (approximately 1½" wide, shown on peach washcloth):
Ch 5, sl st in first ch to form ring.
Row 1: Ch 5, in ring make 3 dc, ch 1, 3 dc [= shell].
Row 2: Ch 4, turn, in ch-1 sp of shell make shell [= 3 dc, ch 1, 3 dc in same sp], ch 2, in ch-5 sp make shell.
Row 3: Ch 1, turn, make shell in ch-1 sp of shell; ch 2, sk ch-2 sp, dc in first dc of nxt shell; ch 2, make shell in ch-1 sp of shell [= 2 ch-2 sps between shells].
Row 4: Ch 4, turn, shell in shell; ch 2, sk 2 dc, dc in third dc of shell, ch 2, dc in nxt dc; ch 2, shell in shell [= 3 ch-2 sps].
Row 5: Ch 1, turn, shell in shell; ch 2, sk ch-2 sp, (dc in nxt dc, ch 2) 3 times; shell in shell [= 4 ch-2 sps].
Row 6: Ch 4, turn, shell in shell, ch 2, sk 2 dc in shell, dc in third dc; (ch 2, dc in nxt dc) 3 times; ch 2, shell in shell [= 5 ch-2 sps].
Row 7: Ch 1, turn, shell in shell; (sc in nxt ch-2 sp; in nxt ch-2 sp make shell) 2 times, sc in nxt sp, ch 2, shell in shell.
Row 8: Ch 4, turn, shell in shell, ch 2, in nxt ch-2 sp make shell.

REPEAT ROWS 3–8 seven times for washcloth, or length desired, except omit row 8 when making final triangle. After final row 7 make (ch 5, 2 sc in nxt ch-4 sp) across length of lace to row 1. Fasten off.

Medium Lace (approximately 3½" wide, shown on peach hand towel):
NOTE: In this pattern the **Band** on the left is made by repeating parts called *Side A* and *Side B*; the **Triangle** on the right is formed by increasing the ch-2 sps by 1 sp in each row.
Row 1: Ch 16 loosely. Dc in fourth ch from hook, dc in nxt ch, ch 2, sk 2 ch, in nxt ch make dc, ch 2, dc [= "V" sp]; ch 2, sk 2 ch, dc in nxt 3 ch, ch 2; sk 2 ch, in nxt ch make 3 dc, ch 1, 3 dc [= shell], ch 2, dc in same ch.
Row 2: Triangle—Ch 1, turn, in ch-2 sp make shell [= 3 dc, ch 1, 3 dc in same sp], ch 2, in ch-1 sp of shell on row below make shell; Band-*Side A*—ch 2, sk ch-2 sp, dc in nxt 3 dc, ch 1, in "V" sp make shell, ch 1, dc in nxt 3 dc.
Row 3: Band-*Side B*—Ch 3 [counts as first dc], turn, dc in nxt 2 dc, ch 2, in ch-1 sp of shell make "V" sp [= dc, ch 2, dc], ch 2, sk ch-1 sp, dc in nxt 3 dc, ch 2;

Triangle—shell in shell, ch 2, sk 2 dc, dc in third dc of same shell, ch 2, shell in shell. [2 sps between shells at this end of row].

Row 4: Ch 1, turn, shell in shell, (ch 2, sk ch-2 sp, dc in nxt dc) 2 times, ch 2, shell in shell; rep Band-*Side A* as in row 2.

Row 5: Rep Band-*Side B* as in row 3; shell in shell, ch 2, sk 2 dc on shell, dc in nxt dc of same shell, (ch 2, dc in nxt dc) 2 times, ch 2, shell in shell. [This end of row will form triangle with same number of ch-2 sps in each direction. On this row there are 4 sps on each side. On each row the number of sps will grow by 1.]

Row 6: Ch 1, turn, shell in shell, (ch 2, sk ch-2 sp, dc in nxt dc) across Triangle including first dc of shell, ch 2, shell in shell; rep Band-*Side A* as in row 2.

Row 7: Rep Band-*Side B* as in row 3; shell in shell, ch 2, sk 2 dc on shell, dc in nxt dc of same shell, (ch 2, dc in nxt dc) across Triangle but not in first dc of shell, ch 2, shell in shell.

Rows 8–11: REPEAT ROWS 6–7 until there are 10 ch-2 sps on each side of Triangle.

Row 12: Ch 1, turn, shell in shell, (sc in nxt sp, shell in nxt sp) across Triangle, (sc in nxt sp) 2 times, ch 3, shell in shell; rep Band-*Side A*.

Row 13: Rep Band-*Side B*; shell in shell.

Row 14: Ch 1, turn, shell in shell; rep Band-*Side A*.

Row 15: Rep Band-*Side B*; shell in shell, ch 2, sc in ch-1 sp below.

Row 16: Ch 1, turn, shell in ch-2 sp, ch 2, shell in shell; rep Band-*Side A*. **REPEAT ROWS 3–16** for length desired, except final Triangle should end with row 12. Fasten off.

For 3½"-wide *Medium Lace* on hand towel, make 7 Triangles with 10 ch-2 sps on each side of triangle. For 4"-wide large-sized lace on bath towel, make 8 Triangles with 14 ch-2 sps on each side of triangle.

For **FINAL ROW** of lace on both sizes, end with row 12. Fasten off.

Potpourri Pocket

Using directions for *Medium Lace*, make a Band/Triangle of 20 ch-2 sps and end with row 12; [rows 13–16 will not be used]. Fasten off. Make a second one the same size but do not cut thread. To join, place them together with both pieces right-side up and shells matching. Ch 1, turn; sl st loosely and evenly across last row of Bands; at Triangle make approximately 9" of ch sts and leave a 15" tail. Cut thread. Weave ch through ch-2 sps nxt to shells at outside of Triangle to form pocket; use tail of thread to sl st loosely across first row of Band. Finish. Insert bag of spicy fragrances. Weave ⅛"-wide ribbon through ch-2 sps in Band and tie in a bow.

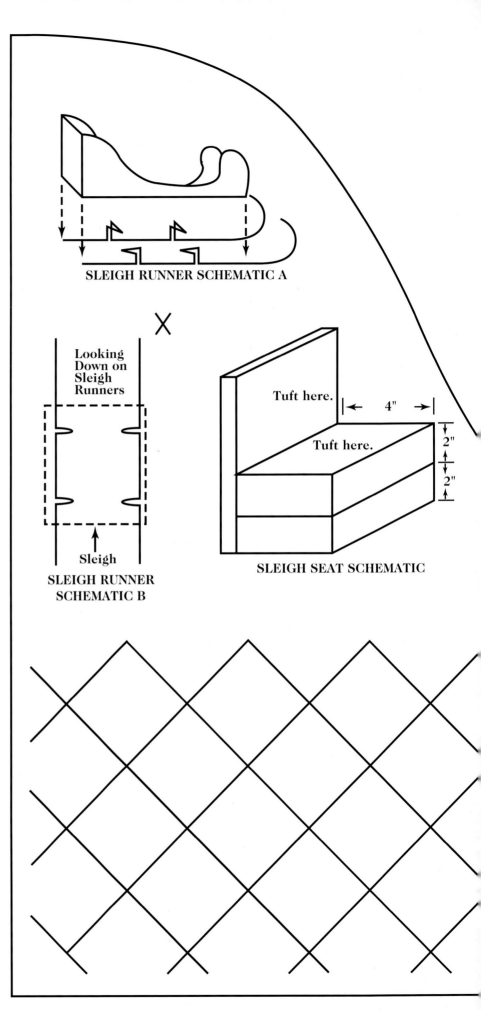

SLEIGH RUNNER SCHEMATIC A

Looking Down on Sleigh Runners

Sleigh

SLEIGH RUNNER SCHEMATIC B

Tuft here.

4"

Tuft here.

2"

2"

SLEIGH SEAT SCHEMATIC

Victorian Sleigh

Materials:

Cardboard box **or** corrugated cardboard **or** mat board and duct tape to make sleigh shape (**Note:** Model box measures 12¼" x 8½" x 10½" tall.)

One 10" x 12" x 1¼" piece STYROFOAM brand plastic foam (for seat back)

Two 4" x 8" x 2" pieces STYROFOAM brand plastic foam (for seat)

1 yd. 44/45"-wide burgundy velour **or** Doe Suede

2 squares black felt

3 yds. ½"-wide off-white braid (for trim)

2 yds. black velvet fabric tubing (**Option:** Use gold or silver if available.)

Purchased decoration of your choice (for side of sleigh)

2 jingle bells   2 wire coat hangers
Pliers with cutters   Tacky glue
Straight pins   Hand-sewing needle
Thread   Scissors
Putty knife **or** dull table knife
Utility knife   Hot glue gun

Note: Styrofoam® was not developed to be heated and may give off unhealthy fumes when heated to a high temperature. Use tacky glue when gluing Styrofoam®—do not use hot glue gun.

1. Adjust pattern at parallel lines, if necessary, to fit box you are using. Trace outline onto box and cut box to sleigh shape, using utility knife. Ends of sleigh are straight across. (**Note:** If making sleigh from cardboard, cut two sides by pattern. Cut 8½" x 10½" rectangle for back. Cut 8½" x 5½" rectangle for front. Cut 8½" x 12¼" rectangle for bottom. Tape pieces together using duct tape.) Pin burgundy fabric around two sides and front of box, leaving ¾" at bottom to turn under sleigh base and back. Trim to fit curves at top of sleigh. (**Note:** Braid will cover raw edges.) Spread tacky glue under fabric, gluing fabric to three sides of sleigh. Pin fabric to back of sleigh, leaving ¾" of fabric to turn under at bottom and enough fabric to come up over back at top of sleigh and down approximately 3" over seat back. Glue back in place but leave free over seat back. Line inside of sleigh with fabric, leaving back unlined. Glue to secure.

2. To make seat back, cut single piece Styrofoam® to fit entire back side of sleigh. (**Note:** Model seat back was cut 9¾" x 7¾".) Place seat back in sleigh. Stack two 4" x 8" x 2" pieces one atop the other for seat, trimming pieces if necessary to fit into sleigh. Seat will be 4" deep, 4" tall, and 8" wide. (**Note:** Model was not trimmed.) Glue two pieces Styrofoam® together, using tacky glue. Mark seat level on seat back. Remove Styrofoam®. Trace diamond shapes onto seat back above seat line and onto top of seat. Score foam ⅛"–¼" deep along traced lines, using putty knife or dull table knife. Cut fabric squares for diamond shapes, cutting each square approximately 3/16" larger all around than diamond shape. To "tuft" seat back, place one fabric square over one diamond shape in seat back, leaving top row of seat back until later. Press edges of fabric square into scored grooves, using dull knife or putty knife. When entire seat back has been tufted in this manner, place Styrofoam® into sleigh. Bring fabric covering back of sleigh over top and, trimming as you tuft, press fabric into top row of diamonds, beginning at center and working toward sides. For seat, cut fabric to cover front of seat and first row of diamonds at front edge of seat. Pin fabric around front side of seat until first row of tufting is completed. Glue front with tacky glue. Tuft remainder of seat top as for back and place seat into sleigh.

3. To make runners, remove hook from each coat hanger, using pliers with cutters. Bend each coat hanger as shown, referring to Sleigh Runner Bending Pattern and noting measurements given with pattern. Slide velvet tubing over each wire. Tack jingle bell at each front runner tip. Set aside.

4. To make lining, cut black felt to fit on floorboard of sleigh and secure to floorboard with tacky glue. Cut black felt to fit bottom of sleigh. Set aside.

5. Use hot glue or tacky glue to attach braid around top edges of sleigh and down back corners, referring to photos on page 50 for placement. Glue band of braid around lower edge.

6. Glue ¾" overlapping fabric to bottom of sleigh. Use hot glue to attach runners to fabric on bottom of sleigh. Cover bottom with black felt, trimming out for runner supports.

7. Glue purchased greenery or other decoration of your choice to side of sleigh.

VICTORIAN SLEIGH PATTERN

SLEIGH RUNNER BENDING PATTERN

1½"
1½"
← 5½" → ← 7" →   11"

Three Carolers

Materials:

2 small magazines, the size of *Readers Digest* (for small caroler)

2 medium magazines, the size of *Good Housekeeping* (for medium caroler)

2 large magazines, the size of *Life* (for large caroler)

Three 4" STYROFOAM brand plastic foam balls

White gesso sealing agent

Paintbrushes: small liner, medium

Yarn, one 3.5-oz. skein **each** in three different colors of your choice (for hair)

3 purchased crochet doilies: one 9", one 12", one 15"

Acrylic paints, colors: flesh, black, white, rose

Two 12-oz. cans spray paint in color of your choice (for magazine bodies)

One ¼" dowel, cut into three 10" lengths

Lightweight construction paper **or** old sheet music (for carol book pages)

Heavy construction paper **or** lightweight cardboard (for hands, sleeves, and cover of carol book)

1⅔ yd. 1½"-wide ribbon in color of your choice (for bows)

Transfer paper and pencil

Blush and applicator   Masking tape

Paper-cutting scissors   Stapler and staples

Straight pins   Hot glue gun

Note: Please read all instructions carefully before beginning. Materials listed will make three carolers: one small, one medium, and one large.

Option: The book cover can also be made from Christmas cards or wrapping paper. If you wish to dismantle carolers for storage after holidays, do not permanently attach sleeves to bodies. Simply separate pages at shoulder level and insert sleeves into body. If sleeves do not feel secure, fasten them inside body with straight pin or piece of tape. To store, remove pins or tape, gently slide sleeves from body, and fold sleeves, book, and hands flat. Heads can be removed as well, along with doilies and bows, for easy storage.

1. Remove outside covers from magazines and all thick advertising pages throughout. Fold each magazine page three times, as indicated in Illustrations 1–4, creasing each fold with finger. Fold each page until entire magazine is folded. Repeat for remaining magazines.

2. Glue two magazines of same size together to form each body, placing spines toward center of body, using hot glue gun, and being careful not to put glue on top half of spines. On top half, put glue on folded pages only, leaving center area of spines unglued so that dowel may be inserted. Let dry. Spray-paint bodies, using several coats to cover completely and allowing to dry thoroughly between coats and after final coat.

3. Put glue on top 2" of one dowel piece and insert dowel piece into one Styrofoam® ball to make caroler's head. Using medium paintbrush, paint ball with at least two heavy coats gesso, allowing to dry between coats. When ball is completely dry, use medium paintbrush to cover with flesh-colored acrylic paint. Let dry. Use transfer paper and pencil to mark mouth, eyes, and nose. Paint features, using small liner brush. When features are dry, apply a small amount of blush to cheeks. Repeat for remaining carolers.

4. Place hand pattern atop heavy construction paper and trace around perimeter of pattern. Flip pattern to trace second hand. **(Note:** Pattern must be flipped to achieve one right and one left hand.) Trace pair of hands for each caroler. Cut out. Paint top side of each hand up to dotted line on pattern, using flesh-colored paint and medium paintbrush. Let dry.

5. Place sleeve pattern atop heavy construction paper and trace around perimeter of pattern. Cut two sleeves for each caroler. Bring two straight edges of each sleeve together and, being careful not to crease folded side, tape edges together using masking tape. Spray paint sleeves, using same paint and brush as for body and being sure to spray up into lower portion of inside of sleeves. Cover completely, using several coats of paint and allowing to dry between coats and after final coat.

Note: The easiest way to paint sleeves is to hang each by its point on clothesline. Portion covered by clothespin will not show on finished caroler.

6. Insert a hand into each sleeve end at taped side and attach, using hot glue gun.

Note: Be sure thumb is at top of each hand.

7. To finish smallest doll's sleeves, turn back 2" on pointed end, cut approximately 1" off point, and staple remaining inch to body. To finish medium doll's sleeves, turn back 1½", cut off ¾", and staple to body. To finish largest doll's sleeves, snip point off but do not turn back. Staple to body.

Note: Attach sleeves for each caroler 1"–1½" below top folded edge of magazine body.

8. There are many ways to make carolers' hair. Smallest caroler shown has short curls, largest has long curls with both ends glued to head, and medium-size caroler has blond "tassels." All hair is attached using hot glue gun. To make each long curl, cut four lengths yarn, each 60" long, and fold in half. While holding one end firmly, twist other end as tightly as you can. Bring ends together, dividing in middle with one finger and keeping taut. Hold ends together firmly and remove finger. Yarn will twist into curls. Tie ends with short piece of matching yarn. You will need approximately 25 curls to cover head. To make each short curl, cut two lengths yarn, each 48" long, and fold in half. Follow instructions for making long curls. You will need approximately 60 short curls to cover head. For bangs, make shorter curls. To make tassels, wrap yarn around three fingers approximately 15 times, tie in middle, and clip ends. You will need approximately 40 tassels, attached close together, to cover head.

Option: Yarn can be braided and wrapped around head, made into pigtails or ponytails, etc. Length and thickness of curls can be varied by using different amounts and lengths of yarn. Experiment to achieve desired effect.

9. Lay crochet doily over top of body, insert dowel through center hole of doily, and push down until head sits on top of body. Make bows from ribbon and attach one at neck of each caroler with straight pin.

10. To make carol books, cut three 5" x 3" rectangles from heavy construction paper and fold in half. Paint words *Christmas Carols* on front cover of each book, using liner brush. Cut nine 4½" x 2½" rectangles from lightweight construction paper to make pages. Fold pages in half and staple at fold to cover, using three folded pages for each book.

11. Glue book in each caroler's hands, referring to photo on page 52 for placement.

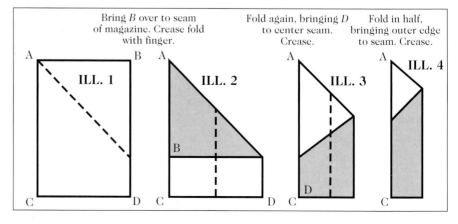

Bring *B* over to seam of magazine. Crease fold with finger. ILL. 1

Fold again, bringing *D* to center seam. Crease. ILL. 2

Fold in half, bringing outer edge to seam. Crease. ILL. 3

ILL. 4

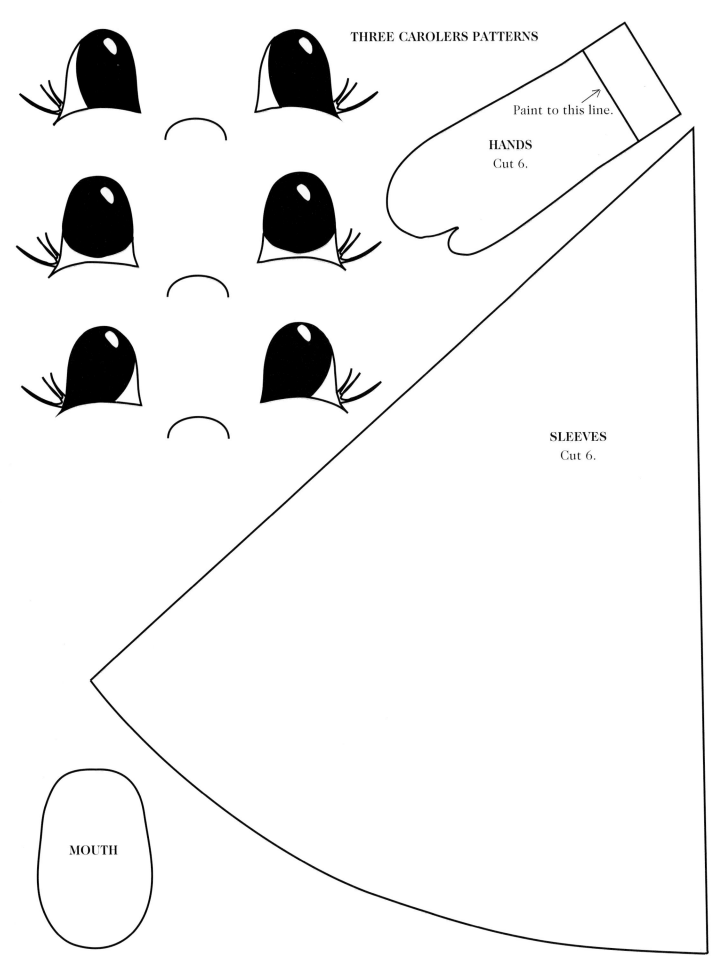

THREE CAROLERS PATTERNS

Paint to this line.

HANDS
Cut 6.

SLEEVES
Cut 6.

MOUTH

FESTIVE TABLES

With every square inch of the house now decorated and the tree festively trimmed with the finest ornaments, it is time to focus on the holiday table, which will serve as the background for wonderful meals that will be shared during this holiday season. Table decorations are as important as the meal itself, and many a hostess has whispered that an imaginative table theme turned an average meal into an event.

Whether you prefer formal or informal dining, this chapter presents table decorations for both. If you are lucky enough to have Christmas dishes, use them and make your color scheme enhance your china. If you are searching for a second set of dishes but prefer not to have a seasonal look, purchase clear glass ones and use them with all of your holiday linens.

You may find, as others have, that a Christmas brunch, luncheon, or tea is a thoughtful gift for your friends. Established as an annual event, your gathering will be anticipated each year as a highlight of the season. Select your best linens, polish the silver, create an enchanting centerpiece, prepare a sumptuous feast, and enjoy having your friends as your guests. It can also be a present to yourself!

Let your imagination guide you as you review the following pages and choose a festive table for the holidays.

FESTIVE TABLES

For the Entire Family

Setting a handsome holiday table is rewarding, not just for the compliments received from friends and family but for the wonderful memories that are created when delicious meals are shared in beautiful surroundings.

Greet early risers at your house with a festive table set for breakfast. The "wake-up" bright primary colors used for this sewing project are favorites at the holiday season. A tea cozy, table runner, hot pad, and egg cozies make up this group of breakfast-time delights. This cheery set uses

fabric and readily available sewing notions cleverly combined to create a charming collection of breakfast accessories! Use the fabric colors suggested or choose your own favorites to match the decor of your home.

One of the most ingenious accessories designed for holiday decorating is a wooden cone that can been easily and inexpensively made and used again and again as a foundation for various decorating themes. The traditional apple stack, topped with a pineapple, is constructed using a base such as

Above and right—With today's new sewing machines, appliquéing is a snap and the finished linens are durable enough to withstand machine washing. Use your handmades and enjoy them during this holiday season without the worry of extensive time spent hand laundering linens.

this. We have included directions so you can make your own wooden base and enjoy using it year-round. In summer, brighten up the breakfast table with a lemon and lime stack, touched with daisies picked from your garden. This idea works well for the Christmas holidays if you replace the flowers with apples, oranges, or seasonal berries. Use a variety of small gourds to assemble a centerpiece that can be used for Thanksgiving and beyond. Our Victorian-style centerpiece, far right, designed for use at a holiday brunch, is fashioned around a plastic foam cone and uses silk roses, ribbons, and grapes with silk greenery. These supplies are commonly available in most crafts stores. If you want to use your centerpiece throughout the year, use silk ivy for the base and make your ribbons decidely Christmas. After New Year's, replace the holiday ribbon with a satin ribbon and you will have a romantic topiary tree to keep on your buffet table. Many craft stores carry lovely artifical birds and bees that could easily be worked into this arrangement. This would be spectacular in all white for weddings and bridal showers.

Above and right—Use your imagination and try new flowers and fruits throughout the year. If you plan to use fruit that will perish easily, dip it in acrylic floor wax, let dry, and then use it in your centerpieces. The wax will seal the fruit and make it last longer. Remember, the fruit is no longer edible after you have sealed it in wax.

When the members of your family gather for Christmas dinner at your house this year, treat them to an extraspecial meal and set the table with a colorful centerpiece and matching gift-box place cards made just for the occasion. You can use these table decorations year after year; and if you're having a dinner party for friends, you can give the wooden place cards as personalized party favors. A glimpse at these cards will remind your guests of the lovely time shared at your holiday get-together.

If you are a lucky parent with grown children and have a large extended family, try using a different ribbon color for each branch of the family. Your son will be delighted to see his family represented with a royal blue bow on each of their place cards, while your daughter might prefer her packages painted with a crimson bow. Paint your grandchildren's birth dates on the back of theirs for a personal touch.

For a real surprise, make a set of package place cards for your bridge-playing friends and paint their packages using hearts, diamonds, clubs, and spades for the background. Ribbons will be perfect painted in red or black, alternating with each card.

Supper-club friends will enjoy birthday package place cards set beside their plates on their special day. How about using this same pattern and painting the packages black for that dreaded fortieth birthday party? You will have fun using this package idea throughout the year for those special gatherings you host.

Salt-flour dough makes sculpting easy as you design your own fruit for the holiday centerpiece shown above. This arrangement,

Above—*Miniature fruit and artificial greenery make this centerpiece easy to assemble and convenient to store. Adjust the fruit selection to fit the size of the tree you plan to use.*

when stored in a dry place after Christmas, will last for years. The artificial greenery makes a foundation for your handmade fruit. Have fun with this one and enjoy sculpting; each piece will have a unique shape and color.

These little fruits enhance round topiary trees for year-round use. Simply cover a round plastic foam ball with greenery, and then follow the directions for placing fruit on the tree. Turn to page 79 for another use of salt-flour dough.

Above—Each member of the family will enjoy seeing his or her place card reappear each Christmas. As the family grows, add packages to remind you of the precious gift of each one.

For the Kids

The children in our lives make Christmas special. From the time the first box is unpacked from the attic, their eyes sparkle and their faces shine as each decoration is carefully lifted from the tissue paper and put in its place for the holidays. They want to touch everything and show it all to you, time and time again, with renewed excitement each time. So it is with our generation, experiencing Christmas with our senses and recalling memories.

Although there are several ideas presented for children to craft under your supervision, this fabric gingerbread house is for you to make and for them to enjoy! Creating memories is what Christmas is about.

When recalling favorite holidays past, the gingerbread cottages our grandmothers and great-grandmothers made at Christmastime come to mind. The baking of the gingerbread for these intricacies warmed the whole house with the wonder of this favorite of all seasons. These delicate masterpieces had a certain way of taking us far, far away, to a magical fantasy land made of lollipops, candy canes, and ice cream snow. The fabric *Gingerbread Cottage*, made of muslin and adorned with felt, trim, and beads, will provide hours of crafting fun and will make a beautiful display piece throughout the holiday season. The added wonder is that when it comes time to pack away the seasonal decorations, this project will fold flat for storage.

Your children will want to be involved in the decorating this year if you encourage them to have a party with neighborhood friends to show off their handwork. Establish a tradition of letting the children make easy-to-do felt trees and decorating them with anything their hearts desire. Be sure that glue, sequins, and ribbons are plentiful for an afternoon of decorating fun.

Right—Select hard candy, lollipops, gum drops, and artificial trees to landscape your creation. Be sure to choose candy that children can eat safely. Purchase plenty or you may see your winter wonderland disappear bite by bite!

Fun Felt Trees are made simply by cutting out two trees and gluing them together at the edges, except at the trunk. After the youngsters have decorated the trees to their satisfaction, place the handiwork over a plastic cup and secure with ribbon for displaying.

For the busy room mother or teacher, this easy-to-make project is perfect for that last-day-of-school Christmas party! Colored construction paper may be substituted for the felt, and the children can cut decorations for their trees from wrapping paper scraps. In just one fun-filled craft period, the class can create a forest of paper evergreens.

If you are looking for a project to use for a special time with your child or grandchild, spend a wonderful afternoon together making snowmen for this Christmas charmer. The easy-to-use salt-flour dough recipe is great for kids and adults alike. The dough is shaped, baked, and painted; and the baked figures are then easily assembled into festive holiday centerpieces. Of course, you don't have to stop with "Frosty." Just use your imagination to create a variety of other popular holiday figures,

Left—Crafts don't have to be complicated to bring great satisfaction, as evidenced by the smiling faces of these crafters enjoying a day of holiday fun!

Below—A host of "Frosties," perched on a silk evergreen wreath, stand guard around the large holiday candle. Made with three salt-flour dough balls, a tiny hat, and a yarn scarf, these guys will be fun for kids to make.

from Santa Claus to Rudolph! Display them throughout your home during this jolly season and enjoy the warmth and cheer they spread, even on the snowiest winter afternoon!

For fun after the holidays, encourage your young ones to make their favorite animals using this same technique. Then place them on a candle ring for use on the family kitchen table.

Another favorite thing to make using this recipe and technique is Easter eggs! Children can make hundreds of them using the basic rolled shape. Painting them is such fun! Fill a petite basket with them for a delightful centerpiece in the spring. Be sure and make the Easter Bunny to go with your egg collection. Keep your shapes simple and you will enjoy the crafting fun.

FESTIVE TABLES

For Special Guests

Hosting Christmas parties and family gatherings is an important part of our holiday celebrations. For those times, we spruce up the house, put out decorations, plan menus, and set the table with our finest tableware. For crafters, the planning that goes into these events begins months in advance and is as much fun as the parties. And what wonderful opportunities to show off fine skills at stitching and handwork. Featured here are a variety of ideas for holiday tables that are certain to delight special guests.

"Simply elegant" describes the beautiful *Feathered Christmas Star* quilt. Rich fabrics in an assortment of prints and solids have been artfully combined to create this spectacular and eye-catching design. Destined to become a family favorite that will be treasured from generation to generation, this piece includes classic quilting patterns mixed with a variation of the well-known feathered-star pattern to form a striking, unforgettable small quilt you will be proud to display in your home. If you're feeling generous this holiday season, you may choose to give it to a cherished friend who shares your love of this American needleart form. Personalize the quilt with your name and the date on the back using a permanent fabric marker or embroidery stitches. There are small fabric labels made especially for quilters who personalize their quilts that are sewed to the backs of finished quilts. Look for them at your local quilt shop or fabric store.

Right—A lovely quilt centerpiece, made with traditional greens and reds, is all that is needed to elegantly enhance an antique table and heirloom dishes.

Above—When setting a festive table, use a centerpiece that echoes the colors of your place mats and china. Carry out the color theme with everything you put on the table for a rich look your guests will remember.

Add a new sparkle to holiday dining by using your own hand-crafted touches. Holiday meal-time magic begins with a dining table transformed by cross-stitched place mats adorned with musical instruments associated with Christmas. Attention to color and detail makes these true masterpieces of stitchery. The border is created by adding two single rows of cross stitching in a floss color that matches the fabric.

Setting a festive table need not be limited to the dining room or breakfast nook. Tables throughout your home provide lovely space for holiday decorating. When the area of your home calls for a more formal look and dressy fabrics, use the elegant taffeta tablecloth and metallic grapes duo shown on page 84 for an impressive decorator look.

Fabric stores offer a large variety of taffetas, including lovely pastels, rich jewel tones, and

some English plaids, at afford-
able prices. With careful planning, you can create a dressy
round cloth that is suitable for a
small tea table or a foyer table as

Above right and right—
*Beautiful eyelet wreaths
double as napkin rings on
your holiday table and can be
presented to guests as a remembrance of the dinner party. Use
your creativity in adorning
them and make each one
different for an interesting look.*

shown. Used over a solid cloth, this versatile piece will be admired wherever you place it.

When the tablecloth is finished, use the taffeta, lamé, and crepe scraps to make clusters of grapes for use around candles, punch bowls, or in arrangements alone. These easy-to-assemble fruits will add a sparkle to your entertaining.

If you love country through and through and metallic fabrics are not appropriate for your cozy home, this ensemble can be made with cotton fabrics in your favorite country prints. Use light cottons and Cluny lace for the cloth and make the grapes from cotton scraps. Display your grape clusters in a grapevine basket and use calico ribbon bows for accents.

When the Christmas season rolls around, it is time to get out your best hand-crocheted tablecloth to place on the dining room table for holiday dinners. If you have inherited your grandmother's lovely handwork, use the cloth and tell your family and friends the story of its origin. Always launder the cloth immediately after use to insure its beauty for years to come.

Following in your grandmother's footsteps, you can create your own heirloom piece by using the simple instructions given for the tablecloth pictured here. Worked in a repeating pattern, this covering will accommodate any size table. Continue to crochet until the piece reaches the size. By beginning today and working on and off at your own pace throughout the year, you can finish this elegant piece in time for your next Christmas gathering!

Above—Sometimes a simple color scheme can create the most elegant look for holiday decorating. This two-tone fabric and lace tablecloth, assembled with squares joined by lace, makes a grand statement for the entryway in your home.

Above—Select a bright green or red undercloth for your Lacy Table-cloth. *The intricate crochet stitches will be showcased if there is a sharp contrast between the crochet and the undercloth.*

Bells & Holly Breakfast Set

Materials:

1½ yds. 44/45"-wide white solid fabric
½ yd. 44/45"-wide green solid fabric
¼ yd. 44/45"-wide red solid fabric
½ yd. 44/45"-wide red mini-dot fabric
¼ yd. **each** 44/45"-wide yellow solid and yellow print fabric
1 pkg. Coats Bias Corded Piping, Art. M. 951P, color 128A Atom Red
2 pkgs. Coats Double Fold Bias Tape, Art. M880P, color 128A Atom Red
1 spool **each** Coats Rayon Machine Embroidery Thread, Art.D.63, colors: 1 2 8 Red, 177 Kerry Green, 182 Spark Gold
1 spool **each** Coats Dual Duty Plus Thread, Art. 210, colors: 1 White, 128 Red
1 yd. Pellon® Wonder-Under® Transfer Web
1 yd. Pellon® fleece
1 plastic bone ring (knitting supply)
Scissors
Pencil
Sewing machine
Iron
19 small red beads (optional)

Note: Please read all instructions carefully before beginning. A ¼" seam allowance is included in measurements and pattern pieces. Appliqué pieces do not require seam allowance.

Preparation:

Tea Cozy—Cut one cozy front and two lining pieces from white solid, two cozy pieces from fleece, one from red mini-dot for backing, and one 4" x 50" strip, pieced as needed, from green solid for ruffle.

Runner—Cut two 14" x 33" rectangles from white solid, one 14" x 33" rectangle from fleece, and two 4" x 20" strips from green solid for ruffles.

Egg Cozy—Cut one front from white solid, one back from red mini-dot, two linings from white solid, and two fleece pieces for each cozy.

Hot Pad—Cut one 8½" square from white solid for front, one 8½" square from red mini-dot for back, and two 8½" square fleece pieces.

Appliqué:

Trace appliqué shapes onto paper side of Wonder-Under®. Cut and fuse to fabrics as noted, following manufacturer's instructions for fusing.

Tea Cozy—Two bells, one bow, and six leaves

Runner—Four bells, two bows, and six leaves

Egg Cozy—Two leaves each

Hot Pad—One bell, one bow, and three leaves

1. Fuse leaves to green solid, bell piece *A* to yellow solid, bell piece *B* to yellow print, and bell piece *C* to red solid. Fuse bow piece *A* to red solid, and bow piece *B* to red mini-dot. Fuse bow pieces *C* and *D* to red solid. Cut out shapes along tracing lines.

2. Arrange appliqué pieces on front of Tea Cozy, Runner, Egg Cozy, and Hot Pad, referring to photo on page 70 for placement. Fuse shapes in place.

3. Using rayon thread in machine and bobbin, set machine to narrow satin stitch (as narrow as you can comfortably handle) to appliqué. Use green thread for leaves, gold for bells, and red for bows.

4. Working from bottom to top, begin appliquéing with pieces that lie under others.

Assembly:

Use white Dual Duty Plus in machine and bobbin.

Tea Cozy—Fold green strip in half along lengthwise edge, placing right sides of fabric together. Sew across short ends, trim corners, turn, and press. Gather along raw edge to make ruffle. Baste fleece piece to wrong side of each lining piece. With right sides together (fleece to outside), sew lining pieces together. Trim fleece seam allowance close to stitching line to eliminate excess bulk. Baste 16" length red piping along edge of cozy front with raw edges even. Baste ruffle over piping, leaving ¼" at bottom edges. (**Note:** Ruffle will start and end ¼" from bottom edge.) Sew cozy front to cozy back with right sides together. Clip curves, turn right-side out, and press. Slip lining into Tea Cozy, matching raw edges and side seams. Baste along raw edge and bind raw edge with double-fold bias tape.

Runner—Make two ruffles as for Tea Cozy. Baste 14" length red piping to each short end of runner. Baste ruffle over piping. Baste fleece to wrong side of backing. Place backing and runner with right sides together and sew along all four sides, leaving 4" opening along one long side for turning. Clip corners, turn right-side out, and press. Slip stitch opening closed.

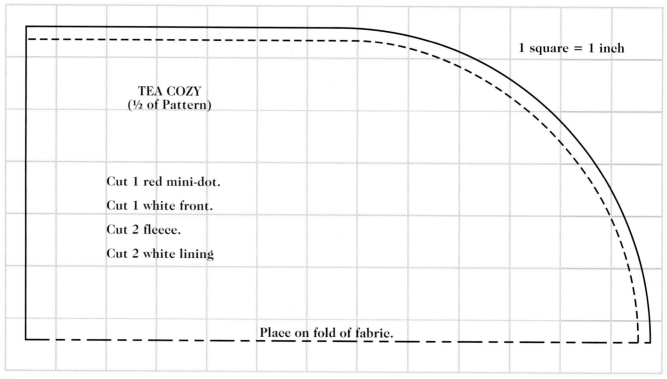

TEA COZY
(½ of Pattern)

Cut 1 red mini-dot.

Cut 1 white front.

Cut 2 fleece.

Cut 2 white lining

Place on fold of fabric.

1 square = 1 inch

Egg Cozy—Assemble as for Tea Cozy, eliminating green ruffle.

Hot Pad—Baste double layer of fleece to wrong side of red mini-dot square. Lay Hot Pad front atop fleece, aligning at edges. Baste close to edge around perimeter of Hot Pad. Bind Hot Pad with double-fold bias tape. Attach ring to top corner, using red Dual Duty thread.

All pieces—Stitch beads to items as desired, using red Dual Duty thread and referring to photo for placement.

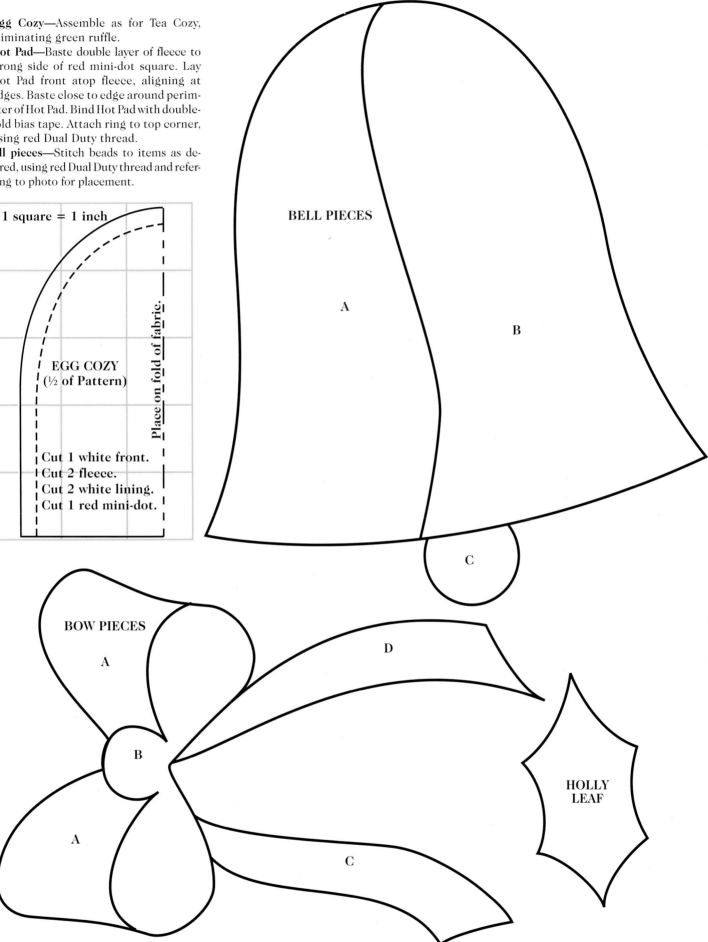

1 square = 1 inch

EGG COZY
(½ of Pattern)

Place on fold of fabric.

Cut 1 white front.
Cut 2 fleece.
Cut 2 white lining.
Cut 1 red mini-dot.

BELL PIECES

A

B

C

D

BOW PIECES

A

B

A

C

HOLLY
LEAF

Trio of Centerpiece Trees

Grapes & Rosebuds Tree
Materials:

14"-tall x 4" STYROFOAM brand plastic foam cone

1 dozen small pink dried-look silk rosebuds

3 large pink dried-look silk rosebuds

4½ yds. ¾"-wide metallic pink ribbon

6"-long piece pink pipe cleaner (for securing center of bow)

Approximately 160 pieces silk evergreen, 1½"–2" long

Approximately 3 dozen assorted silk leaves

5 bunches rose-colored artificial grapes

8–10 small bunches rose-colored berries

Scissors

Tacky glue

1. Beginning at bottom of cone, push silk evergreen stem ends into cone and glue pieces to secure. Repeat until cone is completely covered.

2. Glue on grapes, rosebuds, leaves, and berries, arranging as desired and referring to photo on page 73 for placement.

3. Cut two pieces ribbon: one 18" long, one 24" long. Glue center of each piece ribbon at top of tree for streamers. Make bow with remainder of ribbon, secure center of bow with pipe cleaner, and glue to top of tree.

Note: Refer to instructions for *Tying a Bow*, page 129, for general instructions for making ribbon bows. Remember to adjust the dimensions given for the project on which you are working.

Lemon Tree
Materials:

Centerpiece cone (**Note:** See instructions for *Centerpiece Cone* on page 89.)

6 lemons

6 limes

2 dozen kumquats

Green shrubbery leaves

1 dozen daisies

1 dozen water picks (optional, available at floral shops)

Note: Because fruits are perishable, this centerpiece should be discarded after four–five days.

1. Place lemons and limes as desired on nails of centerpiece cone, referring to photo on page 73 for placement.

2. Fill in open spaces with green shrubbery leaves and kumquats.

3. Stick daisies in desired position, referring to photo for placement.

Note: To keep daisies fresh longer, insert in water picks and position in place **before** adding greenery.

Gourd Tree
Materials:

Centerpiece cone (**Note:** See instructions for *Centerpiece Cone* on page 89.)

15–18 assorted gourds

Boxwood **or** other greenery of your choice

2 dozen wheat stems (available in craft stores)

Ice pick **or** hammer and nail

Varnish (optional)

Paintbrush (optional)

Note: Gourds are perishable. If picked fresh, they will perish more quickly than if left to dry before picking. Depending on their condition when picked, gourds may last only a week or two or can last up to several months. If you wish to preserve dry gourds for many seasons to come, coat them thoroughly with varnish before using.

1. Using ice pick or hammer and nail, make a hole in one end of each gourd for mounting on nails of centerpiece cone. Place gourds as desired on nails of centerpiece cone, referring to photo on page 72 for placement.

2. Fill in open spaces with boxwood.

3. Stick wheat stems into boxwood in desired position, referring to photo for placement.

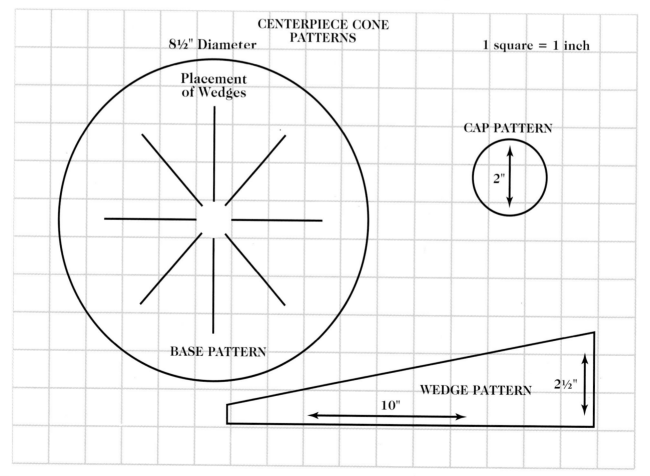

CENTERPIECE CONE PATTERNS

8½" Diameter

1 square = 1 inch

Placement of Wedges

CAP PATTERN

2"

BASE PATTERN

WEDGE PATTERN

2½"

10"

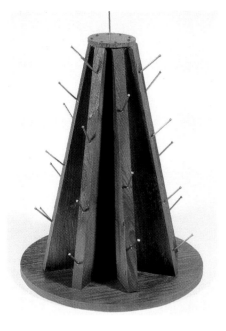

Centerpiece Cone
Materials:

10"-square piece ⅜"-thick plywood (for base)

Eight 3" x 10" pieces ½"-thick pine (for wedges)

3"-square piece ¼"-thick plywood (for cap)

24 #3 finishing nails

29 #4 finishing nails

Hammer

Green spray paint

Pencil

Scroll saw **or** band saw

Radial saw **or** table saw

Note: Materials listed will make one *Centerpiece Cone.*

1. Enlarge patterns as indicated. Cut out patterns. Draw around base pattern on ⅜"-thick plywood and around cap pattern on ¼"-thick plywood; saw out using scroll or band saw.
2. Draw around wedge pattern on each piece ½"-thick pine board and saw out using radial or table saw.
3. Draw wedge placement lines on plywood base, referring to base pattern. Center wedges on lines and nail to base, using two #3 nails for each wedge.
4. Bring tops of wedges together and nail on cap, using eight #3 nails.
5. Spray-paint assembled cone and let dry.
6. Nail #4 nails into wedges, alternating four nails and three nails on every other wedge and staggering placement of nails in a checkerboard fashion. Refer to photo above. Nail one #4 nail into top center of cap. Nails will be used to hold fruit.

Fruit Tree

Materials:

12" STYROFOAM brand plastic foam cone

Artificial boxwood **or** other greenery of your choice

Salt-flour dough (**Note:** Refer to recipe given with *Snowmen Candle Ring on page 92.*)

Whole cloves

Small plastic bag

Ceramcoat® Acrylics by Delta, colors: purple, white, antique gold, bright red, bright yellow

Ceramcoat® Water Base Satin Varnish by Delta

Medium paintbrush

Baking sheet   Tacky glue

1. Pinch off small amounts of dough and shape into apples, pears, and bananas. Insert clove for stem in each apple and pear.
2. Make 15–20 dough balls about the size of a pea for each bunch of grapes. Dip edge of each ball in water (just a dot will do but is needed to make balls stick together) and press grapes together to form bunches.
3. Arrange pieces on baking sheet with no pieces touching and bake at 150°F two–three hours until completely dry, checking frequently to prevent burning.
4. Paint fruits using two coats Ceramcoat® Acrylics, letting pieces dry thoroughly between coats. Paint apples red, bananas yellow, and pears antique gold. For grapes, use purple for first coat and mix purple and white as desired for second coat. Let dry completely. Varnish, applying two coats and letting varnish dry between coats.
5. Cover cone with greenery and glue on fruits as desired.

Wooden Place Cards and Gift Box Centerpiece

Materials:

3½" square ½"-thick pine board for **each** place card

23" length ¼" dowel pin, cut into three 5"-lengths and one 8"-length

6" x 6" x 5"-tall white cardboard gift box

STYROFOAM brand plastic foam, cut to fit inside gift box

2 yds. ⅞"-wide red satin ribbon

3 purchased ribbon bows **or** 1½ yds. 1"-wide Christmas-plaid ribbon and three complementary pipe cleaners (for securing bow centers)

Frosted silk greenery

Red berries

Acrylic paints, colors: red, white, black

Paintbrushes: small, medium

Green fine-point permanent marker

Water-base varnish

Sandpaper

Graphite paper

Pencil

Tacky glue

Scissors

Drill with ¼" bit

Band saw

1. To make each place card, trace pattern onto board, using graphite paper and pencil. Saw out shape and sand. Apply two coats white paint to all sides, using medium paintbrush and leaving bottom unpainted. Let dry.
2. Trace ribbon pattern onto board and paint on ribbon, using two coats red paint and small paintbrush. Let dry after each coat. Mix small amount black paint with red paint and shade areas indicated on pattern, using small paintbrush. Let dry.
3. Apply two coats varnish using medium paintbrush. Let dry.
4. Print name on place card, using marker.
5. To make *Gift Box Centerpiece*, make wood cutouts, following steps 1–3.
6. Drill ¼"–⅜"-deep hole in center bottom of each wood cutout. Insert one end of one dowel in hole in center bottom of each wood cutout and glue in place. Paint dowels white. Let dry.
7. Glue ⅞"-wide ribbon around sides and bottom of box. Glue Styrofoam® in bottom of box. Let dry.
8. Stick greenery stems into Styrofoam®, arranging as desired, and glue stems in place. Let dry. Place dowels with wood cut-outs in desired position, referring to photo on page 75 for placement. Add ribbon bows and clusters of red berries, arranging as desired.

WOODEN PLACE CARD PATTERN

Gingerbread Cottage

Materials:

1⅓ yds. 44/45"-wide muslin (for house)

½ yd. tan cotton fabric (for roof and windows)

⅛ yd. dark green cotton fabric (for shutters)

⅔ yd. 44/45"-wide red-and-white striped cotton fabric

1⅞ yds. ½"–¾"-wide white braid **or** lace (for roof edge)

6" length ⅛"-wide red satin ribbon

3" x 5½" scrap red felt

Green felt scraps **or** miniature greenery

2 yds. Pellon® fleece

6" x 18" piece Pellon® Wonder-Under® Transfer Web

Fifty-two 10mm round red wooden beads

14 white chenille stems

Jingle bell

Miniature wreath

Thread to match fabrics

Hand-sewing needle

Straight pins

White Delta Shiny Stuff™ fabric paint

Cardboard (for house support)

5"-square piece cardboard (for yo-yo pattern)

Compass and pencil   Paper (for patterns)

Pencil   Craft knife

Masking tape   Ruler

Hot glue gun **or** tacky glue

Iron

Sewing machine (optional)

Finished size: 9" x 12" x 17" tall

Note: Please read all instructions carefully before beginning. Cottage and roof will fold flat for storage.

1. Enlarge pattern as indicated or measure and draw on paper. Lines of pattern are seam lines. Layer two thicknesses of fleece and then two thicknesses of muslin. Pin house pattern on top. Sew around, leaving both ends open for turning. Remove pins. Cut out, leaving ¼" seam allowance. Clip corners, turn, and press.

Note: Decorations will be added to house while it is flat.

2. To make roof, cut one 14" x 20" piece and two 11" x 14" pieces from tan fabric. On 11" x 14" pieces, turn under 1" on one 11" side of each piece to form hem; sew. Cut one layer of fleece 14" x 20". Layer fleece, large piece tan fabric right-side up, and two small pieces tan fabric right-side down with hemmed edges in center of large piece. (Refer to Ill. 1.) Sew around outside edges using ¼" seam allowance. Turn and press. **(Note:** This forms pockets for cardboard pieces, which will keep roof stiff.) Cut two 9¼" x 13⅛" pieces cardboard and slip one into each pocket.

3. To make windows, draw four 2" x 3" rectangles on paper side of Wonder-Under®. Fuse to wrong side of tan cotton fabric, following manufacturer's instructions for fusing. Cut out. Fuse in place on house, referring to pattern and photo on page 76 for placement.

4. To make door, draw 3" x 5½" rectangle on paper side of Wonder-Under®. Fuse to wrong side of red felt and fuse in place on house, as in #3.

5. Hand- or machine-quilt horizontal lines ¾" apart for clapboards on house. Quilt around door and windows.

Note: For machine quilting, a walking foot is helpful.

6. Squeeze Shiny Stuff™ on windows to form mullions, following manufacturer's instructions.

7. To make candy-cane door trim, cut 2½" x 20" bias strip from red-and-white striped fabric. With right sides together and aligning raw edges, sew into a tube, using ¼" seam allowance. Turn right-side out. Cut in half to form two tubes and hem one end of each. Stuff each tube with seven chenille stems, bend into candy-cane shapes, and clip off excess stems. Tuck raw edges under at cane bottoms and glue to sides of door.

8. To make yo-yos (they resemble peppermints) for roof, mark 4½"-diameter circle on cardboard and cut out. Mark forty-eight circles on back of red-and-white striped fabric, using pencil and cardboard pattern. Cut out. Using ¼" seam allowance and longest machine-stitch length, sew gathering thread around each circle. Pull up threads to form yo-yos, tucking raw edges inside. Tie gathering threads to secure. (Refer to Ill. 2.) Cut two green felt leaves for each yo-yo, using pattern if desired. Attach yo-yos to roof with hot glue, gluing two leaves and a red bead in center of each.

Option: Glue purchased, miniature greenery and a red bead in center of each yo-yo. Glue braid or lace around edge of roof.

9. To make shutters (you'll need eight), cut a paper pattern 1½" x 3". For each shutter, pin pattern on doubled green cotton fabric with one layer fleece underneath. Cut out. Sew around each shutter close to edges, leaving 1" opening on each for turning. Turn right-side out. Topstitch edges. Attach shutters to house, using hot glue gun.

10. To make greenery, cut felt scraps into ¾" strips and clip diagonally toward center on both sides of each strip. (Refer to Ill. 3.) Twist to make greens stick out and glue to door and windows, referring to photo for placement. You will need approximately 30" of greenery. Add red bead at each window or use mini-ornaments or charms you already have. Tie red satin ribbon in bow and glue bow and jingle bell to purchased wreath.

Glue wreath to door.

11. To make support for house, cut cardboard front, back, and two sides of house ⅛" smaller all around than house pattern. Use masking tape to tape four cardboard corners together. Sew sides of fabric house together. Slip finished fabric house over cardboard support. Pin or glue top points of fabric sides to cardboard at roof crown. Set roof on top of house.

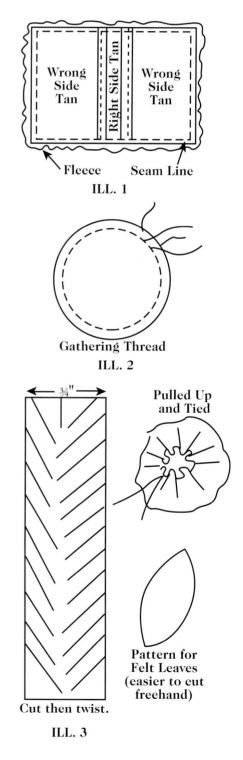

Fleece   **Seam Line**

ILL. 1

Gathering Thread

ILL. 2

¾"

Pulled Up and Tied

Cut then twist.

Pattern for Felt Leaves (easier to cut freehand)

ILL. 3

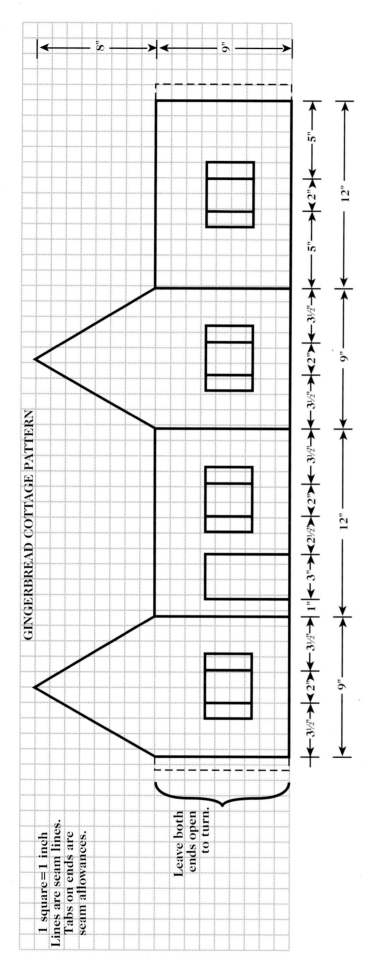

GINGERBREAD COTTAGE PATTERN

1 square = 1 inch
Lines are seam lines.
Tabs on ends are
seam allowances.

Leave both
ends open
to turn.

Fun Felt Trees

Materials:
Two 9" x 12" squares green felt for **each** tree
3" square scrap yellow felt for **each** tree
¾ yd. ¼"-wide red satin ribbon for **each** tree
(for bow at base)
Assorted sequins and decorative trims of
your choice
Children's scissors (with rounded, blunt
tips)
White glue
Pen
3½"-diameter disposable cup for **each** tree

1. Enlarge patterns as indicated. Trace lightly around patterns on felt, tracing two green trees and one yellow star for **each** tree you wish to make. Cut out.
2. Glue tree shapes together, except at trunk, aligning edges. Glue star at top of tree.
3. Decorate as desired.
4. Place over inverted cup and secure with ribbon.

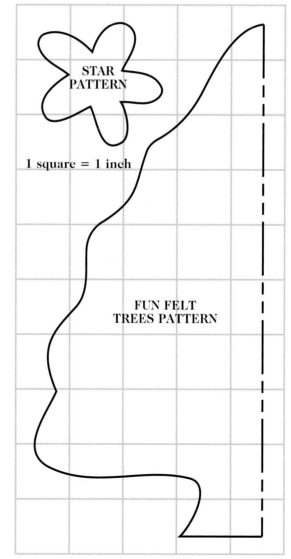

STAR
PATTERN

1 square = 1 inch

FUN FELT
TREES PATTERN

Snowmen Candle Ring

Materials:

8" silk evergreen wreath

Salt-flour dough (**Note:** Refer to following recipe.)

Small hats (available at craft stores)

Scrap of red knitting yarn (for snowmen's scarves)

Ceramcoat® Acrylics by Delta, colors: black, white

Ceramcoat® Water Base Satin Varnish by Delta

Paintbrushes: medium, fine

Baking sheet   Hot glue gun

Dough recipe:

1 c. plain flour

½ c. salt   ½ c. water

Mix flour and salt. Add water and form into a ball. Knead until smooth and about the consistency of biscuit dough. Place mixture in plastic bag to keep moist.

1. To make each snowman body, roll two balls of dough approximately ¾" in diameter. Roll one for head approximately ½" in diameter. Moisten edge of each ball with drop of water and stack together, with smallest dough ball on top.

2. Arrange snowmen figures on baking sheet with figures standing and no figures touching and bake at 150°F two–three hours until completely dry, checking frequently to prevent burning.

3. Paint snowmen figures using medium paintbrush and two coats white Ceramcoat® Acrylics, letting pieces dry thoroughly between coats. Paint hats and facial and body features on snowmen, using fine paintbrush and two coats black Ceramcoat® Acrylics, again letting pieces dry thoroughly between coats. Varnish, applying two coats and letting varnish dry

between coats. Glue on hat and tie on scarf.

4. Glue snowmen to wreath, spacing evenly or as desired.

Feathered Christmas Star

Materials:

½ yd. 44/45"-wide floral-print fabric

½ yd. 44/45"-wide red solid fabric

1 yd. 44/45"-wide ivory solid **or** print fabric (for background)

⅛ yd. 44/45"-wide green print fabric

⅛ yd. 44/45"-wide purple solid fabric

¼ yd. 44/45"-wide green solid fabric (for binding)

1 yd. 44/45"-wide complementary fabric of your choice, cut 34" square (for backing)

34"-square piece lightweight quilt batting

Thread to match fabrics (for piecing)

Quilting thread, colors: natural, green

Plastic **or** paper (for templates)

Silver marking pencil (for marking quilting designs)

¼"-wide masking tape (for marking quilting designs)

Mechanical pencil   Quilting needles

Straight pins   Scissors

Measuring tape   Iron

Finished size: 30" x 30"

A note from the designer: While this quilt is not for the faint of heart, with care and patience, most people can make this beauty. **Note:** Please read all instructions carefully before beginning. Use a ¼" seam allowance throughout. Templates **DO NOT** include seam allowance.

1. To conserve fabric, cut borders first. Cut four 18" x 1" strips from red solid fabric. Cut four 30" x 3" strips from floral-print fabric. Cut three 44" x 2½" strips from green solid fabric. Cut two 14" squares from background fabric,

and then cut these squares on the diagonal to make four background triangles.

2. Trace around all pattern pieces (see page 94) on plastic to make templates. Cut out.

3. Draw around each template on wrong side of fabric as follows, using mechanical pencil for narrow line and leaving at least ½" space between each piece to allow for ¼" seam allowance. Cut out.

Template 1: Cut one from floral-print fabric.

Template 2: Cut eight from purple fabric.

Template 3: Cut four from green print fabric, then turn template over to reverse, and cut four more.

Template 4: Cut seventy-two from background fabric and fifty-six from red solid fabric.

Template 5: Cut eight from red solid fabric.

Template 6: Cut four from background fabric.

Template 7: Cut four from background fabric.

4. To piece center square, join four purple triangles (*Template 2*) to floral center (*Template 1*), following layout shown on *Template 1*.

5. Piece star units as follows to make star block:

a. Make fifty-six squares from red solid fabric triangles and background fabric triangles (*Template 4*), joining long edges of triangles.

b. Make four short pieced strips and four long pieced strips by joining assembled *Template 4* triangle squares and *Template 4* triangles to *Template 5* diamonds, referring to Illustration 1. Join fabric pieces exactly as shown.

c. Make four corner units by combining one short pieced strip and one long pieced strip (made in step 5b) to each of four *Template 7* background-fabric squares, referring to Illustration 2.

d. Make four short pieced strips and four long pieced strips by joining assembled *Template 4* triangle squares and *Template 4*

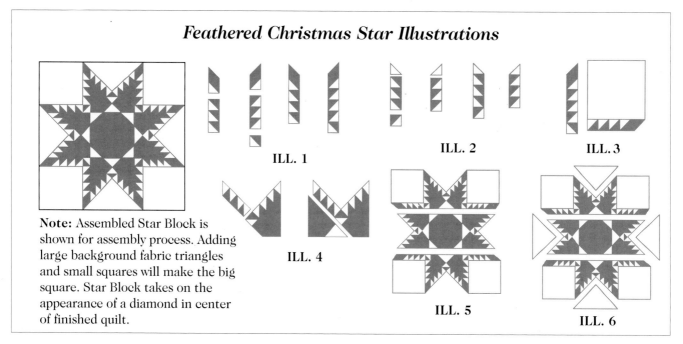

Feathered Christmas Star Illustrations

ILL. 1

ILL. 2

ILL. 3

ILL. 4

ILL. 5

ILL. 6

Note: Assembled Star Block is shown for assembly process. Adding large background fabric triangles and small squares will make the big square. Star Block takes on the appearance of a diamond in center of finished quilt.

triangles, referring to Illustration 3. Join fabric pieces exactly as shown.

e. Sew one purple *Template 2* triangle to one green *Template 3* reverse piece, referring to Illustration 4. Make four star-point units by combining two pieced strips (made in step 5d) to each green *Template 3* piece and one assembled purple *Template 2* and green *Template 3* reverse piece, referring to Illustration 4.

f. Join units together in rows, referring to Illustration 5. Join units exactly as shown.

g. Add side triangles (*Template 6*) by setting the pieces into the four sides, referring to Illustration 6.

Note: You may have to undo a few stitches where point of triangle intersects pieced blocks to get side triangles to lay flat.

6. Attach 1"-wide red strip to each side of star block. Trim ends even with block. Repeat at top and bottom of block.

7. Carefully position two large, background-fabric triangles at each side of star block with red borders. Pin from center out and sew with triangle on bottom so as not to stretch bias edge. Add remaining two large, background triangles to top and bottom of block, pinning and sewing as for side triangles. Press lightly. Trim all edges even.

Note: Adding large, background-fabric triangles will make the square star block take on the appearance of a diamond in center of finished quilt.

8. Attach 30" x 3" floral-print fabric strip to each side of block. Trim ends even. Repeat at top and bottom of block.

9. Press assembled quilt top lightly and mark quilting designs as follows, using silver marking pencil and a light touch. *Design 1* is worked on large, background-fabric triangles. *Design 2* is worked on background-fabric squares (*Template 7*). *Design 3* is worked on small, background-fabric triangles (*Template 6*). Center floral piece and eight green print pieces are quilted ¼" in from edge, using ¼"-wide masking tape as a guide.

10. Place backing fabric right-side down on flat surface. Place batting atop backing fabric and completed quilt top right-side up atop batting. Pin and baste through all layers. Remove pins.

11. To quilt, take small running stitches through all three layers, using a small needle. Use green quilting thread on green fabric pieces and natural quilting thread for remainder of quilting.

12. To make binding, piece 44" x 2½" strips green solid fabric together to make length of at least 130". Fold in half lengthwise with wrong sides together and attach around perimeter of quilt front, aligning raw edges. Sew binding

to quilt, using ¼" seam allowance. Turn binding to back of quilt and blind stitch in place.

13. Be sure to sign and date the back of your quilt with either a permanent pen or in stitches. If you wish to hang your quilt for display, add a sleeve for a dowel or attach a curtain ring for hanging at each top corner.

DESIGN 3

DESIGN 1

DESIGN 2

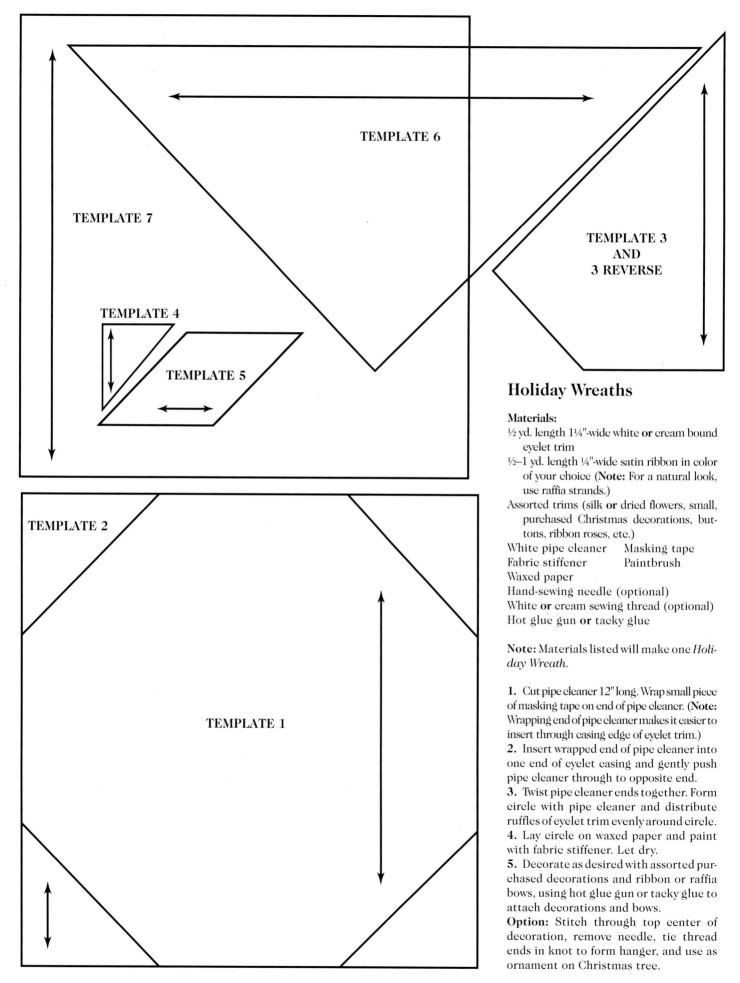

TEMPLATE 6

TEMPLATE 7

**TEMPLATE 3
AND
3 REVERSE**

TEMPLATE 4

TEMPLATE 5

TEMPLATE 2

TEMPLATE 1

Holiday Wreaths

Materials:

½ yd. length 1¼"-wide white **or** cream bound eyelet trim

½–1 yd. length ¼"-wide satin ribbon in color of your choice (**Note:** For a natural look, use raffia strands.)

Assorted trims (silk **or** dried flowers, small, purchased Christmas decorations, buttons, ribbon roses, etc.)

White pipe cleaner   Masking tape

Fabric stiffener   Paintbrush

Waxed paper

Hand-sewing needle (optional)

White **or** cream sewing thread (optional)

Hot glue gun **or** tacky glue

Note: Materials listed will make one *Holiday Wreath.*

1. Cut pipe cleaner 12" long. Wrap small piece of masking tape on end of pipe cleaner. (**Note:** Wrapping end of pipe cleaner makes it easier to insert through casing edge of eyelet trim.)

2. Insert wrapped end of pipe cleaner into one end of eyelet casing and gently push pipe cleaner through to opposite end.

3. Twist pipe cleaner ends together. Form circle with pipe cleaner and distribute ruffles of eyelet trim evenly around circle.

4. Lay circle on waxed paper and paint with fabric stiffener. Let dry.

5. Decorate as desired with assorted purchased decorations and ribbon or raffia bows, using hot glue gun or tacky glue to attach decorations and bows.

Option: Stitch through top center of decoration, remove needle, tie thread ends in knot to form hanger, and use as ornament on Christmas tree.

Musical Instruments Place Mats

Materials:
Four 17¾" x 12¾" pieces 14-count Rich Cranberry Royal Classic Aida

Red thread   Scissors

Measuring tape   Sewing machine

Note: Please read all instruction carefully before beginning. Materials listed will make four *Musical Instruments Place Mats*.

1. Machine stitch ½" in from edge of cross-stitch fabric around perimeter of each piece.

2. Complete cross stitch, following instructions given and referring to illustration for design placement.

Note: From inside edge of machine stitching to outside line of border is twenty spaces on all four sides of place mat. Inside border is twenty-six spaces from machine stitching. There are five spaces between borders. Approximate length of outside border is 197 stitches. Approximate length of inside border is 126 stitches.

3. Pull out threads to machine stitching to fringe.

4. Repeat for remaining place mats.

Mandolin

	DMC	Color
:	471	avocado, vy. lt.
V	470	avocado, lt.
X	469	avocado
Z	937	avocado, med.
●	310	black
O	436	tan
S	434	brown, lt.
II	801	coffee, dk.
3	898	coffee brown, vy. dk.
7	550	violet, vy. dk.
L	603	cranberry
e	601	cranberry, dk.
J	301	mahogany, med.
//	498	red, dk.
bs ecru	ecru	ecru
bs 699	green
bs 702	kelly green

Fabric: 14-count Rich Cranberry Royal Classic Aida from Charles Craft, Inc.

Stitch count: 68H x 90W (motif only)

Design size:

11-count	6⅛" x 8¼"
14-count	4⅞" x 6⅜"
18-count	3¾" x 5"
22-count	3⅛" x 4⅛"

Instructions: Cross stitch using three strands of floss. Backstitch using two strands of floss unless otherwise indicated.

MANDOLIN

Backstitch (bs) instructions:

—   310

•••• ecru (one strand)

∞   699

ⱳ   702

Mandolin

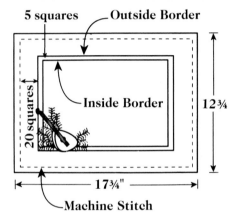

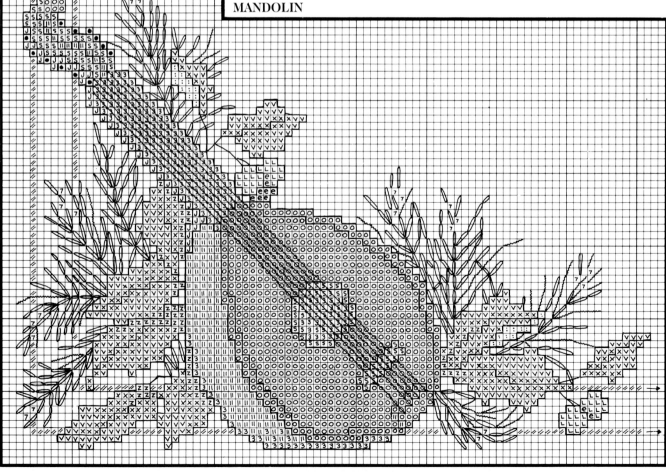

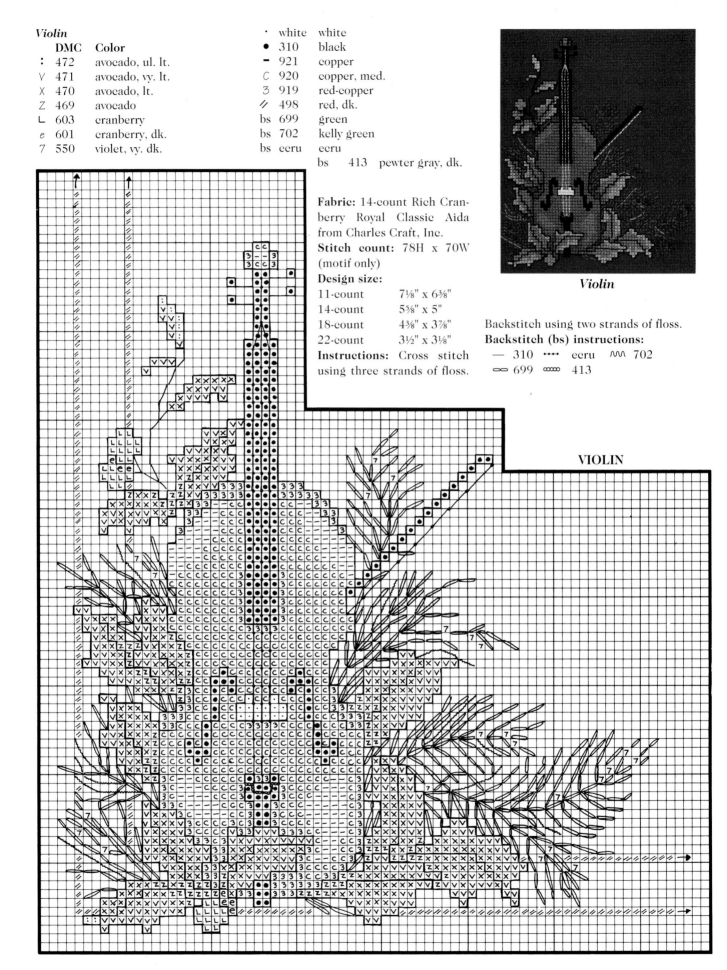

Violin

DMC	Color
: 472	avocado, ul. lt.
V 471	avocado, vy. lt.
X 470	avocado, lt.
Z 469	avocado
L 603	cranberry
e 601	cranberry, dk.
7 550	violet, vy. dk.

· white	white
● 310	black
- 921	copper
C 920	copper, med.
3 919	red-copper
// 498	red, dk.
bs 699	green
bs 702	kelly green
bs ecru	ecru
bs 413	pewter gray, dk.

Fabric: 14-count Rich Cranberry Royal Classic Aida from Charles Craft, Inc.

Stitch count: 78H x 70W (motif only)

Design size:

11-count	7⅛" x 6⅜"
14-count	5⅝" x 5"
18-count	4⅜" x 3⅞"
22-count	3½" x 3⅛"

Instructions: Cross stitch using three strands of floss.

Violin

Backstitch using two strands of floss.

Backstitch (bs) instructions:

— 310 •••• ecru ∿∿ 702
∾∾ 699 ∞∞∞ 413

VIOLIN

Horns

Horns

	DMC	Color
:	471	avocado, vy. lt.
V	470	avocado, lt.
X	469	avocado
Z	937	avocado, med.
7	550	violet, vy. dk.
-	826	blue, med.
o	825	blue, dk.
3	824	blue, vy. dk.
·	813	blue, lt.
II	677	old gold, vy. lt.
C	676	old gold, lt.
+	729	old gold, med.
●	680	old gold, dk.
L	603	cranberry
e	601	cranberry, dk.
//	498	red, dk.
bs	310	black
bs	699	green
bs	702	kelly green

Fabric: 14-count Rich Cranberry Royal Classic Aida from Charles Craft, Inc.
Stitch count: 79H x 88W (motif only)
Design size:

11-count	7⅛" x 8"
14-count	5¾" x 6¼"
18-count	4½" x 4⅞"
22-count	3½" x 4"

Instructions: Cross stitch using three strands of floss. Backstitch using two strands of floss.
Backstitch (bs) instructions:

— 310
∞ 699
〰 702

HORNS

Drum

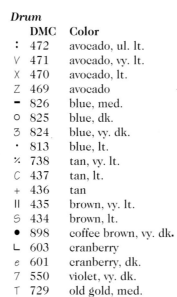

	DMC	Color
:	472	avocado, ul. lt.
V	471	avocado, vy. lt.
X	470	avocado, lt.
Z	469	avocado
–	826	blue, med.
o	825	blue, dk.
3	824	blue, vy. dk.
•	813	blue, lt.
%	738	tan, vy. lt.
C	437	tan, lt.
+	436	tan
II	435	brown, vy. lt.
S	434	brown, lt.
●	898	coffee brown, vy. dk.
L	603	cranberry
e	601	cranberry, dk.
7	550	violet, vy. dk.
T	729	old gold, med.
H	680	old gold, dk.
/	712	cream

∧	822	beige-gray, lt.
//	498	red, dk.
bs	310	black
bs	699	green
bs	702	kelly green

Fabric: 14-count Rich Cranberry Royal Classic Aida from Charles Craft, Inc.
Stitch count: 81H x 83W (motif only)
Design size:

11-count	7½" x 7⅝"
14-count	5⅝" x 5⅞"
18-count	4½" x 4⅝"
22-count	3¾" x 3¾"

Instructions: Cross stitch using three strands of floss. Backstitch using two strands of floss.
Backstitch (bs) instructions:
— 310
∞ 699
⌇ 702

DRUM

Metallic Grapes

Materials:
Nine ⅞" STYROFOAM brand plastic foam balls
Nine 4" squares metallic fabric (**Note:** Lamé or crepe works well.)
Two–three artificial green leaves
Eleven 9"-long pieces 22-gauge wire
Green florist's tape
Pencil

Note: Materials listed will make one cluster *Metallic Grapes*.

1. Insert piece of wire through center of each Styrofoam® ball and pull wire ends even on both sides. Bring wire ends together and twist to secure. Stagger length of wire for each ball.
2. Cover each ball with fabric, pull fabric tight, and wrap securely at base of ball with florist's tape. Then wrap entire stem.
3. Cover all Styrofoam® balls in same manner.
4. Place two wires together and cover with green florist's tape, and then bend around pencil to form grape tendrils.
5. Assemble cluster, beginning with tallest stem and staggering position of each grape. Wrap all stems together with florist's tape to secure, adding grapes and leaves as you go. Use all nine grapes.
6. Arrange clusters as desired to form bunches in a variety of sizes.

Lacy Tablecloth

Crochet Abbreviations:
beg—beginning
ch—chain stitch
dc—double crochet
dtr—double triple crochet
hdc—half double crochet
nxt—next
rep—repeat
sc—single crochet
sk—skip
sl st—slip stitch
sp—space
tog—together
tr—triple crochet

Materials:
Twelve 50-gram balls white DMC Brilliant Crochet Cotton
Size *E* crochet hook **or** size needed to reach gauge of 1 large square = 10" across
Finished size: 50" x 50"
Helpful Hints: Make 25 large motifs and 16 small motifs. Join large motifs 5 rows of 5 each. Join small motifs between large motifs.

Large Square: Ch 6, sl st in first ch to close ring.
Round 1: Ch 6 (count as dc and ch 3), *dc in ring, ch 3; rep from * 5 times, sl st in ch-3 at beg.

Round 2: Ch 3 (count as dc), 2 dc in sp, *ch 3, 3 dc in nxt sp; rep from * around, ch 3, sl st in ch-3 at beg.
Round 3: Ch 3 (count as dc), dc in first dc, * dc in nxt dc, 2 dc in last dc, ch 3 over ch-3, 2 dc in first dc; rep from * ending with sl st in ch-3 at beg.
Round 4: Ch 3 (count as dc), dc in first dc, * dc in nxt 3 dc, 2 dc in last dc, ch 3 over ch-3, 2 dc in first dc; rep from * ending with sl st in ch-3 at beg.
Round 5: Ch 3 (count as dc), dc in first dc, *dc in nxt 5 dc, 2 dc in last dc, ch 4 over ch-3, 2 dc in first dc; rep from * ending with sl st in ch-3 at beg.
Round 6: Ch 3 (count as dc), sk 1 dc, dc in nxt 5 dc, 2 dc tog, *ch 5, dc in ch-4 sp, ch 5, 2 dc tog, dc in nxt 5 dc, 2 dc tog; rep from * ending last rep with ch 5, dc in ch-4 sp, ch 5, sl st in ch-3 at beg.
Round 7: Ch 3 (count as dc), sk 1 dc, dc in nxt 3 dc, 2 dc tog, *(ch 5, dc in ch-5 sp) 2 times, ch 5, 2 dc tog, dc in nxt 3 dc, 2 dc tog; rep from * ending with (ch 5, dc in ch-5 sp) 2 times, ch 5, sl st in ch-3 at beg.
Round 8: Ch 3 (count as dc), work 4 dc tog, *(ch 5, dc in ch-5 sp) 3 times, ch 5, 5 dc tog; rep from * ending with (ch 5, dc in ch-5 sp) 3 times, ch 5, sl st in ch-3 at beg.
Round 9: Ch 1, in each ch-5 sp across work scallop as follows: Sc, hdc, dc, tr, dc, hdc, sc. Rep around ending with sl st in ch-1 at beg.
Round 10: Sl st into tr in center of scallop, then for point, work *ch 6, beg in second ch, work sc, hdc, dc, tr, dtr, then work sc in tr in center of nxt scallop; rep from * around ending with sl st in first ch of ch-6 at beg. Fasten off.

Subsequent Large Motifs: Work as first motif to Round 10. On Round 10, you will start joining large motifs to each other as follows: Ch 6, sl st in corresponding point of previous motif, complete point, join nxt 2 points in same manner. Sk nxt 3 points, join nxt 3 points and so on around. For large motifs on outer edge of tablecloth, you will only join 3 sides of motifs (i.e. join 3 points, sk 3 points, join 3 points, sk 3 points, join 3 points only). For four corner motifs, only two sides will be joined.

Small Motifs: Ch 6, sl st in first ch to close ring.
Round 1: Ch 3 (count as dc), 2 dc in ring, *ch 3, 3 dc in ring; rep from * 3 times, ch 3, sl st in ch-3 at beg.
Round 2: Ch 3 (count as dc), dc in first dc, *dc in nxt dc, 2 dc in last dc, ch 3, dc in ch-3 sp, ch 3, 2 dc in first dc; rep from * ending with sl st in ch-3 at beg.
Round 3: Ch 3 (count as dc), dc in first dc, *dc in nxt 3 dc, 2 dc in last dc, (ch 3, dc in ch-3 sp) 2 times, ch 3, 2 dc in first dc; rep from * ending with sl st in ch-3 at beg.
Round 4 (joining row): Ch 3, work 7 dc tog, *(ch 2, sl st in point on large motif for joining,

ch 2, dc in sp) 2 times, ch 2, sl st in point on large motif, ch 2, work 7 dc tog; rep from * joining around to 4 large motifs altogether, ending row with sl st in ch-3 at beg. Fasten off.

Taffeta Tablecloth

Materials:
2½ yds. 44/45"-wide rose-colored taffeta
16⅔ yds. 1"-wide ivory insertion lace
5½ yds. 1"-wide ivory gathered lace
Thread to match fabric and lace
Pinking shears   Scissors
Tailor's chalk
Sewing machine

Finished size: 60" round

1. Cut thirty-six 10" squares.
Note: Taffeta has a one-way design, so care must be exercised when marking and cutting to make sure all pieces are cut in same direction.
2. Join squares together by stitching wrong side of insertion lace to right side of fabric squares, using ½" seam allowance. Make six rows of six squares. Pink raw edges to prevent fraying. Press seams under.
3. Join two rows of squares, stitching wrong side of insertion lace to right side of fabric squares and using ½" seam allowance. Continue until all rows are joined. Pink raw edges to prevent fraying. Press seams under.
4. Fold cloth into fourths, measure 31" out from folded center, and mark several places on cloth. Using tailor's chalk, draw a line as indicated on illustration to form circle.
Option: If you have trouble drawing a curved line in this manner, you may wish to use this tried-and-true trick for making a perfect circle. Tie a length of string (about 36") to a pencil and trim string to a length of 31" with pencil attached. Use pencil to mark center point at folded center. Unfold fabric, hold end of string securely at center point, and hold pencil upright with string taut. Draw all the way around fabric, keeping string taut, and cut out circle along marking.

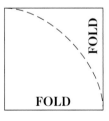

5. Turn narrow hem in raw edge around perimeter of cloth and sew on gathered lace from wrong side.
Note: Gathered edge of lace should be aligned over narrow hem, with right side of gathered lace placed toward stitch, or throat, plate of sewing machine. Working in this manner will make right sides of both fabric and lace face same direction when cloth is turned right-side up.

YULETIDE WEARABLES

That little girl who has grown up seemingly overnight into a blushing young lady is ready for a special holiday dress that only you can make. Elegant velvets and vintage lace in the beautiful Crazy Quilting Jumper echo the times of enchanting Christmases past. Remnants from your workbasket and special snips of lace that you have saved are orchestrated into a jumper bodice that is a showstopper. Coupled with your carefully executed embroidery stitches, the crazy-quilt bodice of the jumper will be a tapestry of memories.

If you are looking for gift ideas, try the lovely Tassel Tree Sweater that requires only a few lark's head knot stitches on a ready-made sweater. This easy-to-make project is perfect for the special friend on your list who looks forward to your handmade gift every year.

Knitters will love to stitch the Child's Cardigan. Two Christmas colors, spiced with teal green, team up for an unbeatable child's sweater that can be worn throughout the winter.

When your holiday parties call for a novelty outfit, try your hand at duplicate stitch to make the lovely Christmas Wreath Sweater. The design lends itself to casual or fancy dressing, determined by the style of sweater you choose.

If you find you need a special holiday outfit in a flash, relax. The Christmas Wreath Sweatshirt is the fast-to-make, fun-to-wear garment for you. Using the new iron-on appliqué technique and some fabric paint, you can make it today and wear it tomorrow!

YULETIDE WEARABLES

Crazy quilts first became popular during the reign of Queen Victoria of England. They were made by using scraps of fabric that were sewn or appliquéd to a foundation cloth. Each seam was then covered with embroidery stitches and decorative details. That haphazard Victorian patchwork influence was the inspiration for these holiday fashions. The jumpers feature rich red velvet skirts topped by crazy-quilt bodices. The bodices were made using velvets, satins, and silks. Adorning the bodices are miniature pearl beads, tiny buttons, and edged satin ribbon. Use the buttons saved from baby clothing for an extraspecial touch.

The key to achieving this antique look is simple: Piece a crazy-quilt section large enough for the bodice pattern to fit on. Add fancy stitches along all seam lines. Next trace the bodice pattern onto the fabric; then machine stitch on this line. Cut out the bodice just outside the stitched line. This will keep your crazy-quilt embroidery stitches from coming apart.

The dresses were made using a commercially available pattern. A crazy-quilt section can be substituted for the bodice of any pattern if the quilting and cutting are done as described. If a more casual look is what you desire, use pretty cottons and floral chintzes.

The jumper bodices feature embroidery done with silk buttonhole twist and six-strand embroidery floss. The buttons are antique pearl and mother-of-pearl. Use old laces and ribbons for a vintage look.

Above and left—Crazy Quilting Jumpers *make wonderful heirloom pieces for little girls. Save buttons and fabric scraps from their baby dresses and use them to embellish these beautiful garments. Perhaps you are fortunate enough to have old buttons left from your favorite childhood dress, or from garments that belonged to your mother or grandmother.*

Right and below—Looking for a quick-to-craft gift? Whip up this Christmas Wreath Sweatshirt in a few hours! Make one for yourself using leftover Christmas-print scraps.

If you think the only place to display a holiday wreath is on a door, think again! Red-and-white candy cane stripes form the ideal background for this beautiful "greenery" circle, created in duplicate stitch on a colorful stockinette-stitch sweater. Of course, every wreath should have a bow. This gold metallic accent provides the perfect finishing touch, completing a design that will allow you to show your stitching skills in breathtaking style.

Duplicate stitch is an easy way to achieve a handmade look without the long hours. It is a simple stitch that duplicates the knit stitch. Be sure to use the appropriate number of floss strands to cover the knitted stitches in the sweater completely. Your friends will think you spent hours knitting!

If you like the *Christmas Wreath Sweater* but find your stitching time running short as the season approaches, you can create a similar look in a fraction of the time using holiday fabric leaves fused to a solid white sweatshirt. Outlined with fabric paint to finish the edges, these "greens" form a project that's faster to finish than traditional appliqué. Completed with acrylic rhinestone holly berries and a large, red ribbon bow, the colorful *Christmas Wreath Sweatshirt,* left, holds extraspecial seasonal appeal!

For the knitter who makes her gifts months in advance, the *Child's Cardigan* on page 106 is a winner. Dress the special little lady in your life in style during the cold winter months in this fashion-plate garment. The girl's sweater combines red and white with teal green, a refreshing departure from the traditional Christmas green, and is a perfect complement to the boy's purchased sweater.

Show your enthusiasm for the holiday season when you use embroidery floss, jingle bells, and a star to transform a basic wardrobe piece into the eye-catching *Tassel Tree Sweater,* also on page 106. You'll love donning this warm holiday-inspired sweater, whether you have worked your set of lark's head knots on a brand-new pullover or an old favorite from your closet.

Above—If your holiday festivities call for a dressier look, this wreath would look wonderful on a solid red or white sweater worn over a black skirt.

Right and below—Repeated quick turns of the hook create a charming holiday favorite, the evergreen tree, on the Tassel Tree Sweater, *right*. An age-old needleart form, knitting was employed to form an eye-catching cardigan that your young miss will enjoy wearing throughout the winter months.

Crazy Quilting Jumpers

Materials:

Purchased pattern (**Note:** Select a pattern with separate bodice and skirt. Refer to pattern to determine amounts of fabric needed for bodice backing and skirt.)

Muslin (for bodice backing)

Fabric (for skirt)

Fabric scraps (for quilt pieces)

Assorted buttons, beads, and seed pearls (for embellishing)

Notions required by pattern (for finishing garment)

Embroidery thread in assorted colors

Hand-sewing needle

Scissors

Sewing machine with zigzag stitch

1. To determine size of area to be quilted, place bodice-front pattern piece atop fabric to be used for backing. Trace around edges of pattern.

2. Place crazy-quilt pieces atop backing fabric in random pattern as desired, leaving ¼" for seam allowances around all edges of quilt pieces and making sure completed crazy-quilt design will be 2" larger than bodice on all sides.

3. Machine-sew crazy-quilt pieces together, beginning in one corner of design and working outward to edges.

4. Embellish seam lines with surface embroidery stitches as desired, referring to stitch illustrations and taking care **NOT** to place buttons, beads, seed pearls, or other embellishments in or near garment construction seam lines.

Note: Placing solid-surface embellishments in or near construction seam lines may interfere with operation of sewing machine.

5. Position paper pattern atop embellished area and trace around pattern to transfer cutting lines to right side of crazy-quilt piece.

6. Zigzag raw edges of bodice **BEFORE** cutting to prevent quilting stitches from fraying.

7. Assemble garment following manufacturer's instructions.

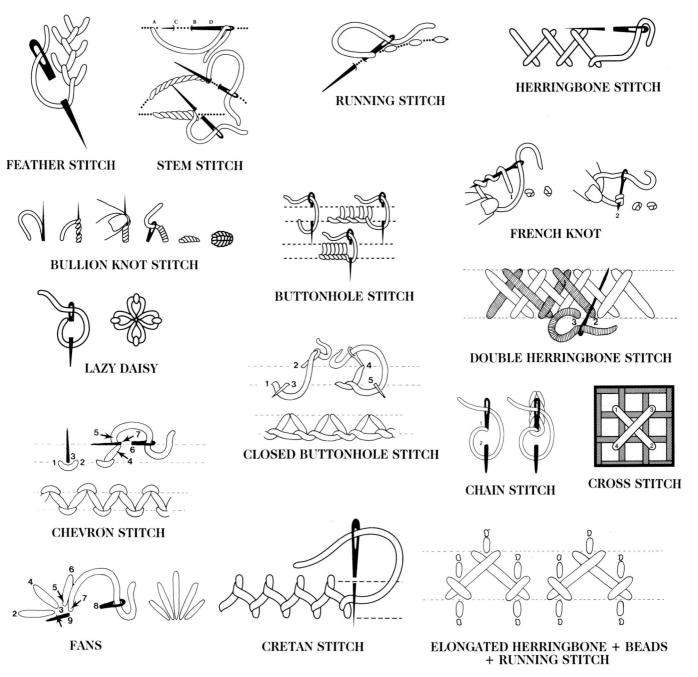

FEATHER STITCH   STEM STITCH   RUNNING STITCH   HERRINGBONE STITCH

BULLION KNOT STITCH   BUTTONHOLE STITCH   FRENCH KNOT

LAZY DAISY   DOUBLE HERRINGBONE STITCH

CLOSED BUTTONHOLE STITCH   CHAIN STITCH   CROSS STITCH

CHEVRON STITCH

FANS   CRETAN STITCH   ELONGATED HERRINGBONE + BEADS + RUNNING STITCH

TOP

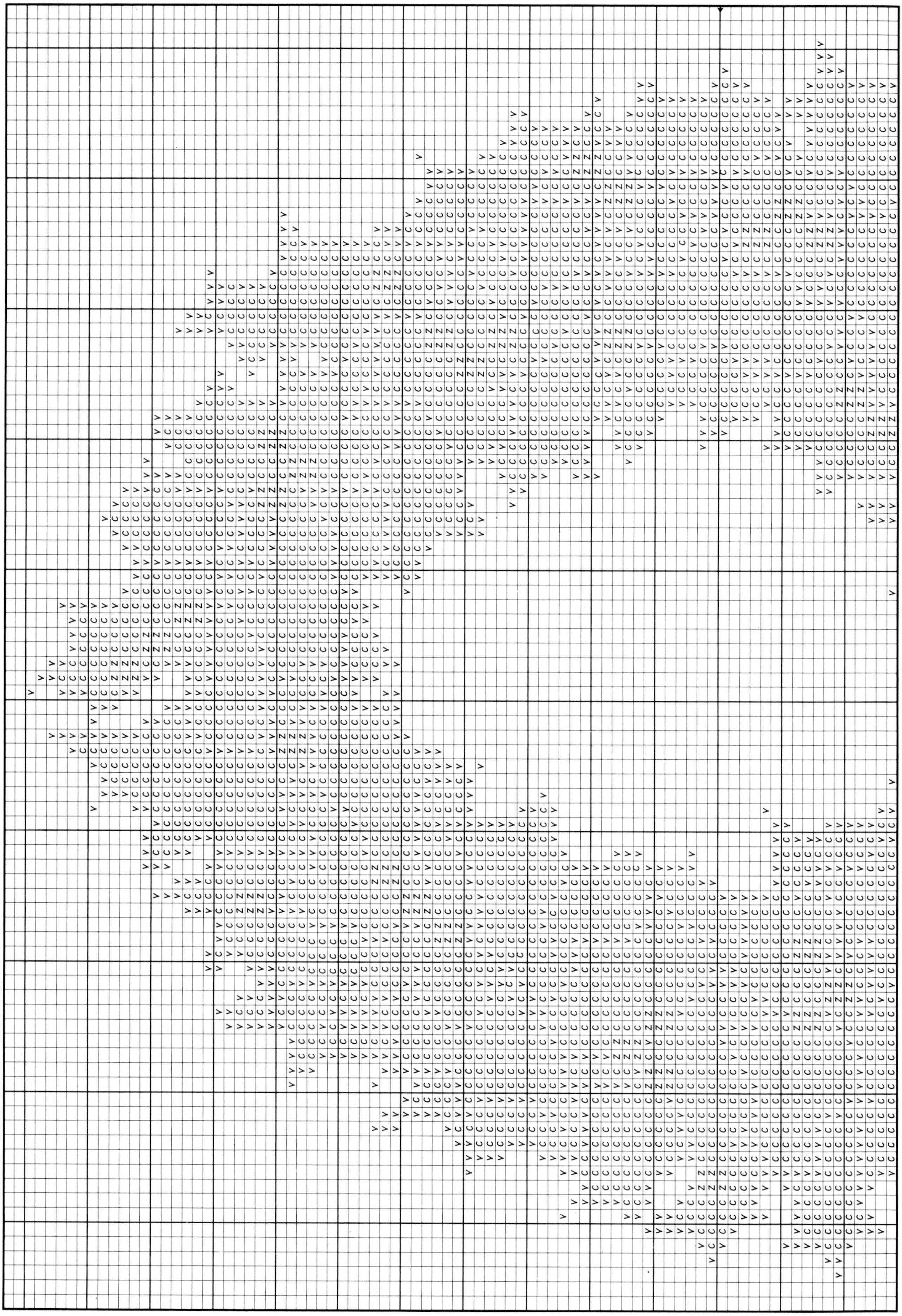

Shaded portion indicates overlap from previous page.

Christmas Wreath Sweater

	DMC	Kreinik Metallics	Color
C	699		green (8 skeins)
B	834		olive, vy. lt. (5 skeins)
		002HL-BF	gold, hi lustre
H	832		olive
Z	321		red
V	701		green, lt. (5 skeins)

Sweater: red-and-white striped pullover stockinette-stitch sweater from *Just CrossStitch®* (12 vertical stitches per inch, 8 horizontal stitches per inch)
Stitch count: 132H x 86W

Instructions: Center design 3" below neckline. Work duplicate stitch using six strands of floss. For better coverage, floss strands should be separated and put back together. Backstitch using four strands of floss.
Note: When blending DMC and Kreinik Metallics, use four strands DMC and two strands Kreinik Blending Filament.

DUPLICATE-STITCH INSTRUCTIONS

Step 1—Thread needle and tie a knot at end of floss. Anchor floss on back of sweater, looping thread several times before beginning. Insert needle from back and bring through to right side of sweater in the center of a stitch.

Step 2—Slip needle under two threads of the stitch above and draw through.

Step 3—To complete stitch, insert needle in hole where stitch began. This represents one square on chart.

DUPLICATE STITCH

Christmas Wreath Sweatshirt

Materials:
Purchased white poly/cotton sweatshirt
¼ yd. **total** 44/55"-wide scraps of five to
    six different Christmas fabrics
Two 5" x 5½" scraps red-and-white candy-
    stripe fabric (optional, for elbow
    patches)
1½ yds. 2"-wide red grosgrain ribbon
    (for bow)
4" piece ⅛"-wide red ribbon (for tying
    center of bow)
¼ yd. Pellon® Wonder-Under® Transfer Web
25 red acrylic rhinestones (for holly
    berries)
1 bottle green shiny fabric paint
Dinner plate (approximately 9" in
    diameter)
Small safety pin
Scissors
Pencil
Hot glue gun
Iron

1. Enlarge patterns as indicated. Iron
Wonder-Under® to wrong side of each
scrap of Christmas fabric, following
manufacturer's instructions for fusing.
Trace assorted leaf shapes on paper side
of Wonder-Under® and cut out.
Note: Model contains 38 leaves.
2. Draw a circle on center front of
sweatshirt, using dinner plate as a guide.
Peel paper from back of each leaf and,
alternating fabrics and colors, place
leaves side by side, overlapping around
circle and referring to photo on page 104
for placement. When satisfied with placement, fuse leaves to sweatshirt, following
manufacturer's instructions for fusing.
3. Outline leaves with fabric paint. Let
dry. Adhere rhinestones as desired around
wreath, using hot glue gun.
4. Make bow from 2"-wide ribbon and
secure in center with ⅛" wide ribbon.
Pin bow to sweatshirt so that it can be
removed for laundering.
Option: For elbow patches, iron Won-
der-Under® to wrong side of red-and-
white candy-stripe fabric, following
manufacturer's instructions for fusing.
Trace elbow pattern on paper side of
Wonder-Under® twice and cut out. Fuse
patches to elbows of sweatshirt, following manufacturer's instructions for fusing, and outline patches, using green
fabric paint. Let dry.
Care: Remove bow from sweatshirt.
Wash sweatshirt on delicate cycle **IN-
SIDE OUT** and hang to dry. **DO NOT**
place in a hot dryer.

Child's Cardigan

Child's Size: 4 (6–8)
Finished Chest Size: 27" (29"–31")
Materials:
Bernat's Berella 4 worsted-weight acrylic
(100 gr skeins): 1 (2–2) skein(s) color no.
8942 white (A), 1 (1–1) skein color no.
8822 dark lagoon (B), and 1 (1–1) skein
color no. 8933 scarlet (C)
One pair **each** 5 and 7 needles **or** size to
obtain correct gauge
Six buttons
Gauge: In St st with larger needles, 5
sts = 1"

Back: With smaller needles and B, cast
on 61 (67–71) sts.
Row 1: K1, *p1, k1, rep from * across.

Row 2: P1, *k1, p1. Rep rows 1 & 2 until 1½"
from beg inc 5 (3–5) sts evenly across last
row—66 (70–76) sts. Then, with larger
needles, work chart 1 repeating last 12
rows until armhole shaping is complete. At
9" (10"–11") from beg, shape armhole: Bind
off 5 sts at beg of next 2 rows, then 1 st each
end every other row 4 times—48 (52–58)
sts. Following chart 2, work even repeating
last 4 rows until 5" (5½"–6") above armhole.
Bind off 13 (14–16) sts, work across next 22
(24–26) sts and leave on holder for back of
neck. Bind off rem sts.
Left front: With smaller needles and B,
cast on 30 (32–34) sts.
Rows 1–2: K1, p1. Repeat rows 1 & 2 until 1½" from beg inc 3 (3–4) sts evenly
across last row—33 (35–38) sts. Then,
with larger needles, work following chart
1 as for back. At 9" (10"–11") from beg,
shape armhole as for back, then continue
front following chart 2 as for back—24
(26–29) sts. At 3½" (4"–4½") from beg,
leave 8 (9–10) sts on holder at neck edge,
then dec 1 st at same edge every other
row 3 times—13 (14–16) sts. Work even
until same length as back to shoulder.
Bind off all sts.
Right front: With smaller needles and B,
cast on 30 (32–34) sts.
Rows 1–2: P1, k1. Complete as for left front,
reversing armhole and neck shaping.
Sleeves: With smaller needles and B, cast
on 33 (35–37) sts. Work in ribbing as for
lower back for 2" inc 7 sts evenly across

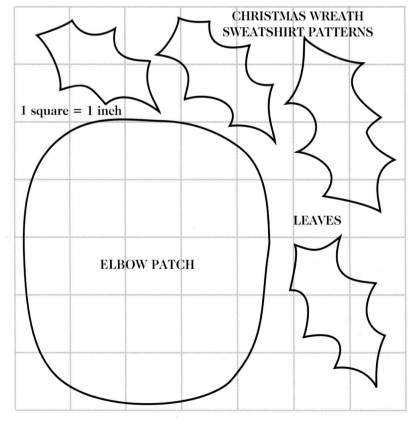

CHRISTMAS WREATH
SWEATSHIRT PATTERNS

1 square = 1 inch

ELBOW PATCH

LEAVES

last row—40 (42–44) sts. Then, with larger needles, work in St st following chart 1 as for back inc 1 st each end every 2½" (2⅓"–2¼") 3 (4–5) times—46 (50–54) sts. Work even until 10½" (12"–13½") from beg or desired length to underarm. **SHAPE CAP** (note that for color pattern, continue working chart 1 until ready to work chart 2 on same row as front and back): Bind off 5 sts at beg of next 2 rows, then 1 st each end every other row until 14 sts remain. Bind off 2 sts at beg of next 4 rows. Bind off rem 6 sts.

Neck band: Sew shoulder seams. With smaller needles and B, work across 8 (9–10) sts from front holder, pick up and k 10 sts on side of neck, work across 22 (24–26) sts from back holder, pick up and k 9 sts on side of neck, work across 8 (9–10) sts from front holder—57 (61–65) sts. Work in ribbing as for lower back until 1" from beg. Bind off all sts.

Buttonhole bands:
Left: With smaller needles and B, pick up and k 69 (75–81) sts. Work in k1, p1 rib as for lower back until band is 1" wide. Bind off all sts.
Right: Work as for left side for ½" ending after a wrong side row. Next row, k on 1 (2–2) sts, (yo, k2 tog, k on 11 (12–13) sts) 5 times, yo, k2 tog, k on 1 (1–2) sts. Complete band as for left side.
Finishing: Set in sleeves at armhole opening. Sew underarm and side seams. Sew buttons opposite buttonholes.

Tassel Tree Sweater

Materials:
Purchased stockinette-stitch sweater, color: solid ivory **or** white
Thread to match
J. & P. Coats 6-strand embroidery floss, colors: 1 skein 6225 light green (L), 2 skeins 6226 medium green (M), 3 skeins 6031 dark green (D)
Ten ⅜" gold jingle bells
Purchased ¾" gold star soft mini-ornament
Hand-sewing needle
Small latch hook
Tracing paper   Pencil
Straight pins   Scissors

1. Enlarge pattern as indicated and trace pattern onto tracing paper. Pin tracing paper pattern to sweater front, centering design. Carefully try on sweater to be sure placement of design is flattering. Mark placement of tassels on sweater with pins and remove paper pattern.

2. To prepare floss, unwind skein and fold entire, nine-yard length in half three times. Cut loops at each end. (**Note:** When finished, you will have a 1⅛-yd. length of eight strands of floss.) Cut floss into 4"-long sections of eight strands each. Repeat for each skein.

3. Begin making lark's head knot tassels, referring to Illustrations 1–4. Begin on bottom row of tree and refer to pattern for color placement. Insert hook where tassel will be (Illustration 1), pointing hook from bottom of sweater toward top (neck). Slide hook under approximately two stitches of knitted sweater. Grasp center of 4"-long section of floss with hook (Illustration 2) and pull floss through sweater, forming a loop. Grasp tails of floss (Illustration 3) and pull them through loop to form tassel, or lark's head (Illustration 4). Trim ends of each tassel, as needed.

4. Tack bells randomly between tassels and tack star at top of tree.

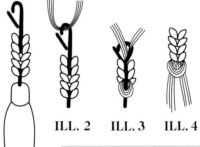

ILL. 2   ILL. 3   ILL. 4

ILL. 1

CHART 1

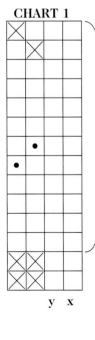

☐ A—White
☒ B—Green
• C—Red

Repeat these 12 rows.

For size	start at
4	y
6	y
8	x

CHART 2

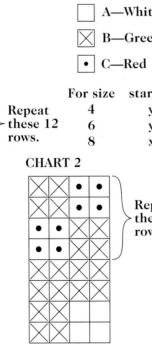

Repeat these 4 rows.

y   x

TASSEL TREE SWEATER			✳D		1 square = 1 inch			
			•M	•L				
		•L	•D	•M				
		•M	•D	•M	•D			
	•L	•D	•D	•M	•M			
	•D	•D	•M	•D	•L	•D		
•M	•L	•M	•L	•M	•D	•M		
•L	•D	•M	•D	•M	•D	•L	•D	
•D	•M	•D	•D	•D	•D	•D	•D	•M

ENCHANTING DECORATIONS

After the stately Christmas tree is adorned in all its glory, turn your thoughts to other areas of your home that need a special holiday touch.

The mantel stands in readiness for jolly Saint Nick and boasts a collection of wonderful stockings just waiting to be filled. Whether you knit, crochet, cross stitch, or sew, there is a stocking for you! If you want to make more than one stocking from a single pattern, simply substitute colors of your own choice for different looks.

The space above the mantel is a perfect place to display small quilts. A simple Log Cabin quilt is featured in traditional red and green Christmas fabrics. Accompanying this design is a stocking made from scraps. In addition, a beautiful Cathedral Window quilt showcases a Christmas tree. Simply fold and stitch squares of fabric to create the "blocks" of this stunning design.

Rounding out the collection of decorations are easy cross-stitch designs that make lovely gifts. These small framed pieces can be made weeks ahead and presented as early gifts so the recipient can display them all season.

ENCHANTING DECORATIONS

ENCHANTING DECORATIONS

Making Great Entrances

Wreaths are so popular that they are being used year-round for decorating needs. The wreath for all seasons below uses silk "dried-look" flowers, a type of silk flower that is sold in most craft stores. These dried-look flowers are perfect to use on wreaths that are displayed in high-traffic areas of your home. Regular dried flowers tend to shed, but these can withstand countless door slams while continuing to hold their shape. The vast variety of colors available makes it easy to color match to ribbons. The simple assembly techniques will make you a pro at wreath making as you craft these for your home or as gifts for special friends.

The designer of the *Classic Christmas Wreath*, right, says her best ideas for craft projects usually come to her when she least expects them. And so it was with the inspiration for this splendid decoration! While shopping in a clothing store, she spotted coordinating paisley and corduroy fabrics with a mixture of patterns and textures she knew would make a unique project. So she set off to a fabric store, where she found these five fabulous materials. Follow her lead and head to your favorite store to begin your search. Then create your own *Classic Christmas Wreath*.

Display this wreath in a protected doorway. The fabric used is beautiful, but not waterproof. Then be prepared for compliments sure to come.

Right—The cloth-covered balls make this wreath great for indoor use. Easy-to-coordinate fabrics allow you to match table linens and tree skirts already in your house.

Left—If you have a friend who shares your love of country, make this wreath in her favorite colors and she can use it all year.

Adorning the Mantel

Not a Christmas morning passes without children scurrying to find their stockings. The magical mysteries of treasures hidden deep in the toe of the stocking fascinate young and old alike. Many families carry on the tradition of hanging these for their children even after they have established homes of their own, and they add more for the grandchildren as they come into the family.

There are many wonderful possibilities for filling stockings. Here is a list of ideas to spark your imagination:
• Golf balls and tees for the golfer
• Cookie cutters for the cook
• Nail polish and emery boards for teens
• Sports cards for athletes
• Embroidery floss for the stitcher
• Baby supplies for the expectant mother
• Fishing lures for Granddad
• Flower seeds for Mom
• Craft supplies for the creative family member
• Recipe cards for Grandma
• Coupons for the shopper
• Decorative soaps and potpourri for an aunt
• Colored chalks for young artists
• Blank audio and video tapes for Dad or teens
• Costume jewelry for Sis
• Stickers for the grandkids
• Herbs and spices for the chef
• Free babysitting coupons for friends
• Perfume samples for Mom

Whether you prefer traditional red and green or you favor the muted burgundy and teal currently popular, you're certain to enjoy the timeless, classic appeal of these "argyle" Christmas stockings. Cross stitched to resemble the ever-popular diamond-patterned socks, these holiday treasures will surely delight you, not only while you're making them but also when that jolly character in red has finished filling them! Begin stitching now and make a pair for yourself and your sweetheart or, if you have children, stitch enough for the entire family! The design can be worked as shown or wrought on a variety of other background fabrics of the same count, allowing you to experiment and choose your favorite colors while maintaining the desired finished size. Select a different color combination to use for each member of your family or make all your mantel adornments alike and take time to add each loved one's name to the cuff. Hang your creations by the chimney with care and rest assured Saint Nick will visit your house on Christmas Eve!

Created completely in stockinette stitch and adorned with double cross stitch and herringbone stitch worked in traditional holiday colors, the stocking shown on page 118 will be a delightful addition to your yuletide decorating. Hang this knitted gift holder in a prominent spot on Christmas Eve and dream of the goodies that will be nestled within it on Christmas morn.

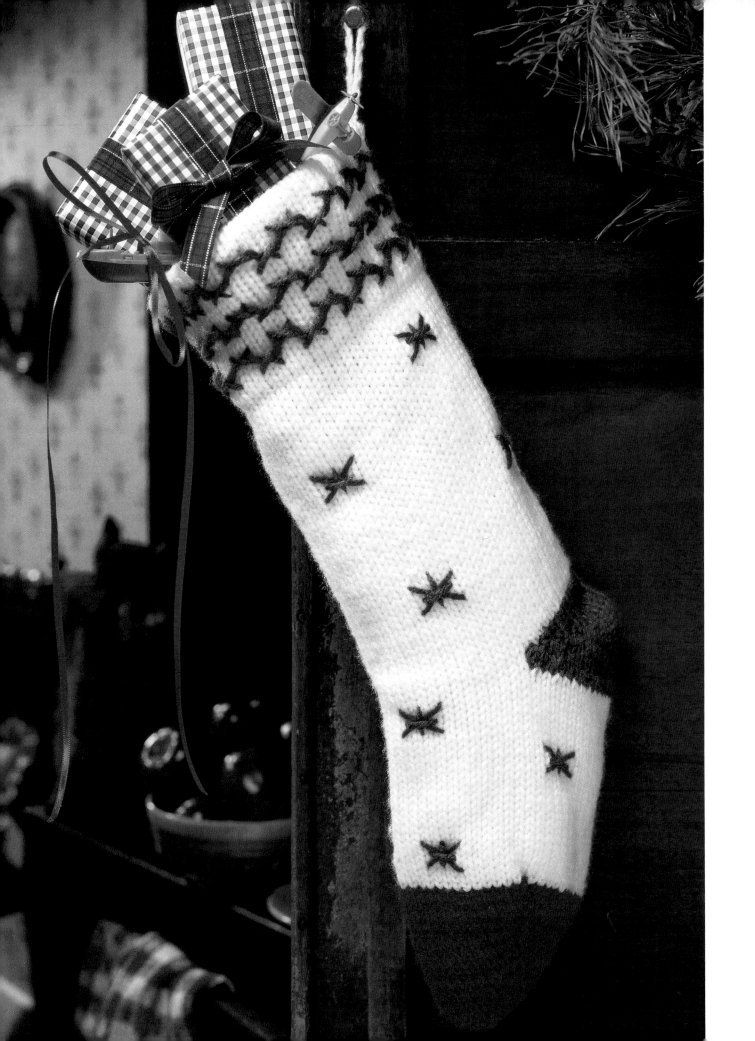

What could be more charming hanging from your mantel? Using wool flannel, an easy-to-work blanket stitch, and simple appliqué techniques, you can create this wonderful *Woolen Santa Stocking* in a short time. When making more than one, you may want to change the colors on the toe and cuff. Try a plaid fabric for a nice touch! A group of stockings can be made by changing the background fabric. Surprise Santa when he drops down your chimney—he will probably leave you an extra treat for this charming tribute!

The age-old art of quilting takes on a festive, holiday look in a size that can be completed quickly. The traditional Log Cabin quilt pattern on page 120 is worked in an assortment of varying calico prints in shades of red and green. Sixteen blocks were stitched for the wall hanging and assembled using a quilted border of holly and bells. Be

Left—Get your knitting needles ready and start this easy-to-make stocking. The simple color patterns makes this fun to knit and quick to finish.

Above—This easy-to-stitch stocking makes use of small scraps of flannel left from your other projects.

Left—Crochet has been a part of our needlework heritage for hundreds of years. It is delicate and charming and perfect for adorning velvet stockings. These bands are crocheted and then attached, making a striking pair of Filet Christmas Stockings.

sure your quilting thread contrasts with your fabric to show off the unique border. Quilt on leftover scrap fabric, experiment with several colors of quilting thread, and select your favorite before completing the quilt. If you are especially fond of quilting, why not share the pleasure and create a priceless remembrance of friends who quilt by organizing a quilt-block exchange?

Above—*The technique used to make the Log Cabin quilt can also be used on a smaller scale to create a beautiful stocking from scraps of leftover fabric. Complete your stocking by adding ribbons with jingle bells tied to the ends.*

Decking the Walls

Watching special Christmas programs each year on television is a special treat, and *Frosty the Snowman* is always a favorite. If you look forward to the annual telling of this enchanting story, you'll enjoy making this adorable wall hanging and capturing "Frosty" for display in your home throughout the season. Though obtaining the materials for much of this adorable wall hanging may require a trip to the fabric store, some of the smaller fabric pieces may already be at your fingertips. Check your sewing box for usable scraps before purchasing new fabric, and then don't be surprised if you catch yourself humming the notes of that well-known Christmas tune as you cut out and machine appliqué the pieces that create this whimsical wall art!

Right—Bright colors make this ideal for displaying in a child's room. The band on "Frosty's" hat and the border colors can be matched to the decor of the room in which this piece will be displayed.

One hundred sixty-nine "windows" in four different colors comprise this *Cathedral Window Quilt*, which features a Christmas tree complete with a gold star at the top. Although called a quilt, this project is actually piecework, with no quilting involved. Achieved by folding and appliquéing the muslin around each separate piece of colored fabric, this creation is sure to become a family keepsake.

Right—Simple folding techniques give this quilt an intricate look. Select a bold fabric for the central tree "windows."

Above and left—Welcome visitors to your festively decorated home with these tangled lights designs. A great way to use scraps from other projects, these designs will appeal to those who prefer a contemporary flavor in their Christmas decorating or who simply like an occasional change from the traditional red and green. Use the table center square on a punch and snack table. Of course, if the dining table at your house is not quite large enough to hold all the grandchildren, you can use this delightful piece to cover an ordinary card table and turn it into an extraordinary kids' table at mealtime. The children will love the bright, splashy colors, and they'll feel extraspecial sitting at their very own holiday table!

I heard the bells on Christmas day
Their old familiar carols play,
And wild and sweet the words repeat
Of peace on earth, good will to men.

Above—*Clever musical notes placed on the staff remind us to enjoy the music of Christmas.*

Left—*The warmth of red print fabrics against a background of white makes this country charmer perfect for a cozy kitchen table.*

This striking red and white *Snowflake Quilt* features an intricate pattern that requires careful piecing. Certain to become a much-noticed accent in your home, this small needleart masterpiece is just the right size for displaying on a wall or for topping a table in unforgettable seasonal style. For year-round use, fashion this design using non-holiday fabric colors of your choice.

Large tolling bells heard from the church steeple in the center of town or tiny ones fastened to tots' hairbows remind us of the wonderful sounds of Christmas. As children, we always associated bells with the holiday season and wondered when tinkling bells would be heard on the roof on Christmas Eve. A cross-stitched design that plays off the old familiar carol "I Heard the Bells on Christmas Day" makes a delightful gift to stitch and present to someone who loves Christmas music. A collection of various bells displayed near the needlework makes a simple yet striking tabletop arrangement. This is a perfect gift for the choirmaster in your church.

The artfully decorated and fragrant evergreeen tree in our homes is always the center of attention. In this cross-stitch design a forest of evergreens on bright red fabric proclaims a greeting of the season—perfect for adding a holiday touch to your foyer.

If you prefer a traditional country look for your Christmas decorating, choose antique green and cream floss colors for your stitching and frame it in a wooden frame with a plaid mat. Using this simple chart, you can achieve a variety of looks by varying the colors and finishing selections.

Above—Red, white, and green, proclaim that it's Christmastime once again in this charming cross-stitch design. Complete your trees with gold stars, and welcome the yuletide season with style.

126

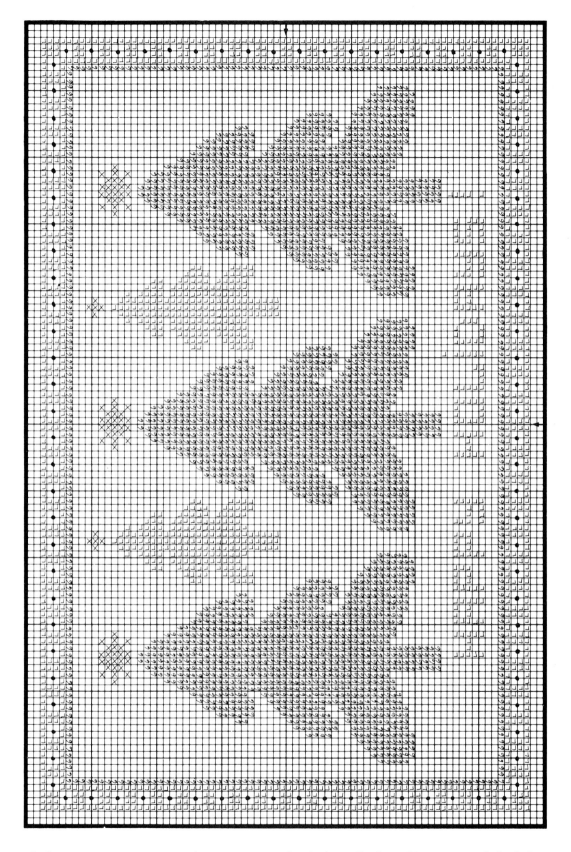

Happy Holidays!

DMC	Color
6 701	green, lt.
L white	white
X 725	topaz

Fabric: 14-count red Aida from Charles Craft, Inc.

Stitch count: 76H x 116W

Design size:

11-count	7" x 10½"
14-count	5½" x 8¼"
18-count	4¼" x 6½"
22-count	3½" x 5¼"

Instructions: Cross stitch using three strands of floss. Make French knots where • appears at intersecting grid lines, using two strands 701 and wrapping floss around needle twice.

I Heard the Bells

DMC	Color
ε 676	old gold, lt.
• 986	forest, vy. dk.
X 304	red, med.
C 844	beaver gray, ul. dk.

Fabric: 14-count ivory Damask Aida from Wichelt Imports, Inc.
Stitch count: 103H x 115W

Design size:

11-count	9⅜" x 10½"
14-count	7⅜" x 8¼"
18-count	5¾" x 6⅜"
22-count	4⅝" x 5¼"

Instructions: Cross stitch using two strands of floss. Attach purchased ribbons above bells with a hot glue gun or tack them with thread at point indicated by *B* above bells. Backstitch bells and staff lines using one strand 844; use two strands 844 for all other backstitching.

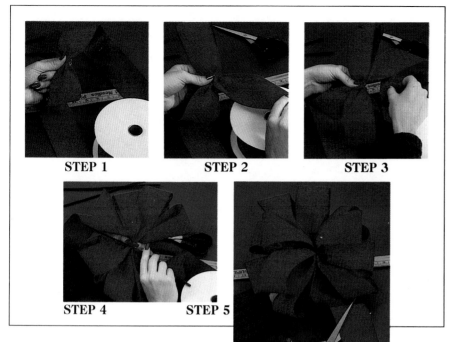

STEP 1　　　STEP 2　　　STEP 3

STEP 4　　　STEP 5

A Wreath for All Seasons

Materials:
16"-diameter straw wreath
2 oz. pkg. natural raffia
3 dried-look silk rosebuds with leaves
9 or more dried, rose-colored globe amaranths
Five 18"-long cinnamon sticks
5 yds. 1¼"-wide print ribbon
6" pipe cleaner to match ribbon
14" florist's wire (for hanger)
Hot glue gun

1. Wrap wire around wreath and twist ends together to make hanger.
2. Separate raffia strands. Glue ends to wreath and begin wrapping around wreath very close together, using two pieces at a time. Glue free ends to wreath and repeat procedure until wreath is completely covered with raffia.
3. Glue one end of ribbon to back of wreath and wrap ribbon around wreath, spacing evenly and referring to photo on page 114 for placement. Cut and glue second ribbon end down. Make bow from remainder of ribbon, using pipe cleaner to tie center and referring to *Tying a Bow* instructions on this page. Set aside.
4. Refer to photo on page 114 and glue cinnamon sticks together, crossing one or two over the others for a fan effect. Tie at center with several pieces raffia. Do not trim. Glue assembled sticks on left-hand side of wreath.
5. Cut rose stems to desired length and glue in place, referring to photo on page 114 for placement. Glue extra leaves on either side, above, and below where raffia is tied to cinnamon sticks.

6. Glue ribbon bow atop raffia where tied at center of cinnamon sticks.
7. Glue on globe amaranths, referring to photo for placement.
8. Loop several pieces raffia and glue above bow. Trim raffia ends to desired lengths.

Tying a Bow

Materials:
5 yds. 2½"-wide red waterproof ribbon
12"-long red pipe cleaner
Yardstick　　　Scissors

Note: Lay yardstick flat on work surface for measuring. You will need both hands to hold ribbon. Refer to photos above.

1. To make first streamer, measure 24" of ribbon (do not cut) and crimp edges together at this point. This crimped area will be center of bow.
2. To make first loop, hold crimped area between thumb and forefinger with streamer hanging down and right (flocked) side facing you. Measure 10" of remaining ribbon, bring to back of center, crimp edges together and twist ribbon so right side is up. This loop will be to the left of the bow's center.
Note: Each time you bring a loop to the center, you must twist the ribbon so that the right side will be up for the next loop.
3. To make second loop, continue to hold center as indicated. Measure 10" of remaining ribbon, bring to back of center, crimp edges together and twist ribbon over so right side of ribbon is up. This loop will be to right of bow's center.
4. Continue making loops on left and right of bow's center until there are six loops on

either side. Always bring crimped ribbon to back of bow.
5. Let second streamer hang down with right side facing you.
6. Secure center of bow (crimped area) with pipe cleaner, twisting tightly.
7. Beginning on one side of center, pull one loop up and one loop down until each loop is in a pleasing position. Repeat for other side.
8. Trim ends of streamers.

Classic Christmas Wreath

Materials:
One 24"-diameter silk evergreen wreath with sturdy wire foundation
STYROFOAM brand plastic foam balls: twenty 1", twelve 2", eight 2½"
2 yds. gold metallic rope cording
1 yd. ⅜"-wide red-and-green metallic striped ribbon
13 metallic gold pinecones (available in craft stores)
½ yd. **each** 44/45"-wide fabrics in five complementary colors and/or prints (**Note:** Cotton paisley, red corduroy, cotton print, green iridescent acetate, and gold satin charmeuse were used for model.)
1 spool 22-gauge craft wire
Wire cutters　　　Scissors
Ruler　　　Hot glue gun

1. Cover Styrofoam® balls with fabrics, mixing fabrics and ball sizes as you go. 1" balls require a 5" square of fabric; 2" balls, an 8" square; and 2½" balls, a 9" square. Cover each ball tightly with fabric square and twist excess to form base at bottom of ball. Twist 4"-length wire around base to secure fabric. Clip wire and fabric tail to approximately 1".
2. Divide wreath into five equal sections. In each section, glue the tail end of a 2½" ball to wreath. Glue another 2½" ball in three of five sections. Randomly glue 2" balls in each section. (**Note:** Some sections will have two 2" balls while others will have one or three.) Glue 1" balls between and to sides of larger balls.
3. Make small, six-loop bow at center of gold rope and twist-tie center with 4"-length wire. Trim wire tails to 1" and glue bow to wreath in between two sections of balls at what will be top of wreath. Tuck and glue remaining gold rope randomly around wreath, referring to photo on page 114 for placement.
4. Make seven-loop bow with two 6"-long streamers from ⅜"-wide ribbon. Twist-tie center with 4"-length wire. Trim wire to 1" and glue ribbon bow to center of gold rope bow.
5. Randomly glue gold metallic pinecones into five sections of wreath.

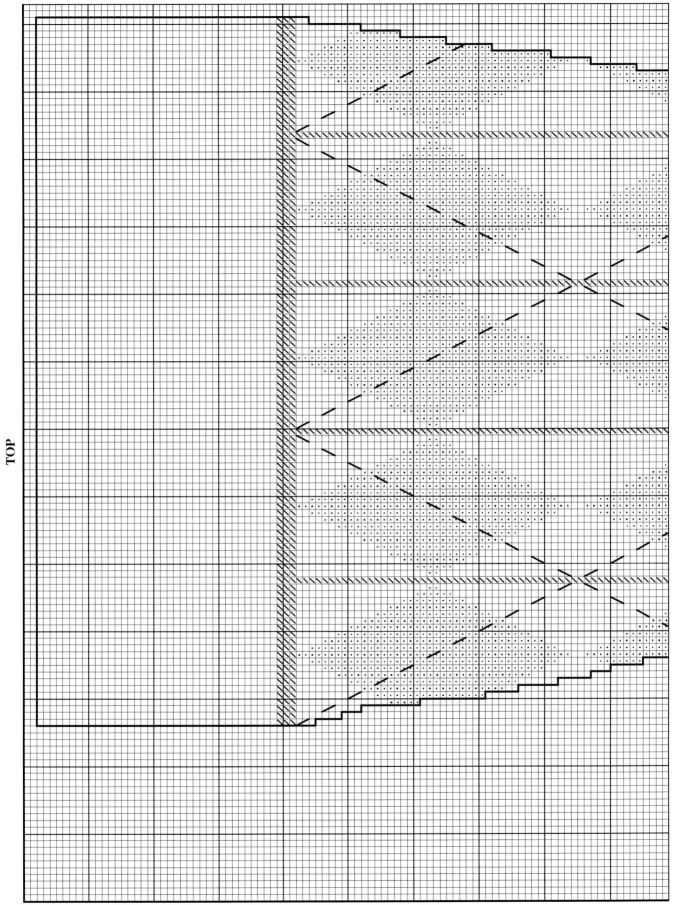

TOP

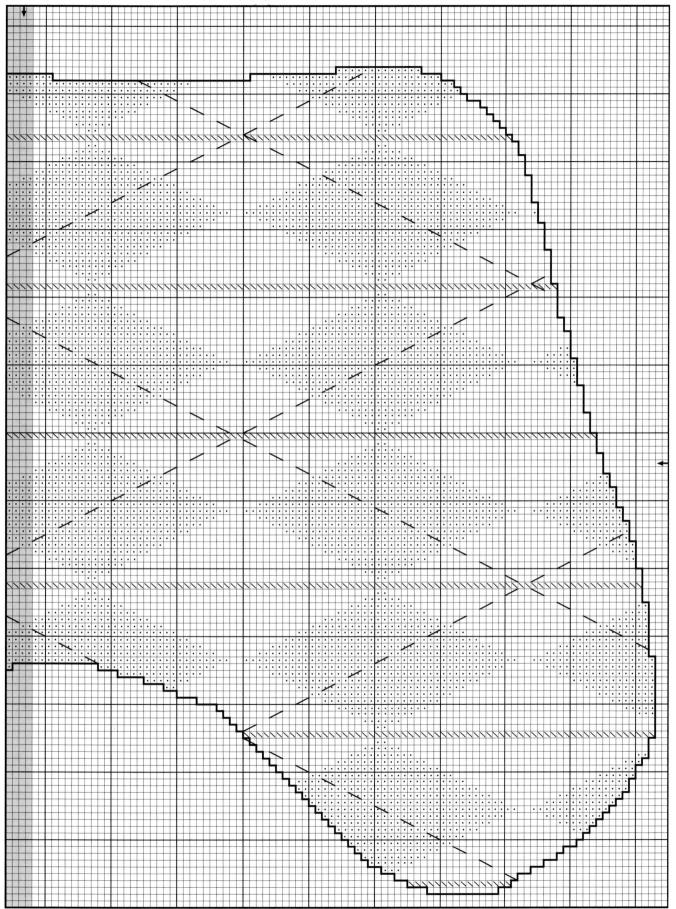

Argyle Stockings

Cranberry Stocking

DMC	Color
∕ 726	topaz, lt.
• 890	pistachio, ul. dk.
bs 002 Balger® #8 gold braid	

Teal Stocking

DMC	Color
∕ 726	topaz, lt.
• 814	garnet, dk.
bs 002 Balger® #8 gold braid	

Fabric: 14-count royal classic rich cranberry Aida or 14-count royal classic deep teal Aida from Charles Craft, Inc.

Stitch count: 190H x 130W

Design size:

12-count	15⅞" x 10⅞"
14-count	13⅝" x 9⅜"
16-count	11⅞" x 8⅛"
18-count	10⅝" x 7¼"

Instructions: Cross stitch using three strands of floss. Backstitch (bs) diagonal lines using 002 Balger®.

Materials:

12" x 16" piece complementary backing fabric for **each** stocking

Two 12" x 13" pieces fleece for **each** stocking

3½ yds. metallic gold piping

½ yd. 44/45"-wide muslin (for lining)

8" piece gold cord for **each** stocking (for hanging loop)

Thread to match each stocking

Water-soluble fabric-marking pen

Tracing paper   #9 needle

Straight pins   Scissors

Sewing machine with zigzag stitch and zipper foot

1. Complete cross stitch following instructions given.

2. Cut away excess fabric from around perimeter of stitched design, leaving 5¾" of fabric at top of stocking for cuff and hem and ½" of fabric around remainder of stocking for seam allowance. Zigzag edges to prevent fraying. Trace outline onto paper and cut out pattern. At top of pattern, mark top of stitched design and 2¾" up from top of stitched design. Flip pattern and trace outline on right side of backing fabric. Trace outline onto two fleece pieces, using water-soluble fabric-marking pen and ending at mark 2¾" up from top of stitched design. Cut stocking shapes from backing fabric and fleece.

3. Baste one fleece shape to wrong side of backing fabric and the other to wrong side of stitched design, aligning toes and heels. Sew gold piping to right side of stitched design around perimeter of design, excluding top of stocking and placing raw edge of piping toward raw edge of fabric. Place front and backing pieces with right sides together and sew around perimeter of stitched design, leaving top of stocking open for turning. Trim, clip curves, turn stocking right-side out, and press.

4. To hem cuff, turn fabric at top of stocking down ¼" toward outside of stocking and ¼" again and topstitch close to turned edge. Sew gold piping around outside top of stocking atop hem, placing raw edge toward bottom of stocking and aligning piping with top edge of fabric. Turn top of stocking down at 2¾" mark. Press.

5. To make lining, trace stocking pattern onto muslin, stopping at 2¾" mark. Cut out lining pieces, cutting top ½" above 2¾" mark. Sew two muslin pieces together as for stocking, leaving top open. **DO NOT TURN LINING RIGHT-SIDE OUT.**

6. Tuck lining into stocking and fold top raw edge of lining under ½" or as needed to align top of lining with top of stocking. Tack lining to stocking around top perimeter, leaving small opening at heel seam for hanging loop.

7. Fold 8" length gold cord in half to form hanging loop and insert ends in opening between stocking and lining. Tack in place. Whipstitch opening closed.

Filet Christmas Stockings

Crochet Abbreviations:	
ch—chain(s)	sl st—slip stitch
dc—double crochet	sp(s)—space(s)
nxt—next	st(s)—stitch(es)
sc—single crochet	tr—triple crochet
sk—skip	
rpt—Repeat * to * number of times indicated	
( )—repeat between ( )s as indicated	

Finished size: Filet measures 2⅞" across, plus edging

Materials:

400 yds. ball Clark's® Big Ball, Size 20 Mercerized Crochet Cotton, color: white

Size 10 steel crochet hook **or** size needed to reach gauge of 11 rows = 2" (**Note:** Three motifs fit one side of 7"-wide top of 14"-long stocking. It is important to change hook size if necessary to reach gauge.)

Helpful hints: For even sts and better tension control, use smooth thread and wind thread an extra time around your little or ring finger. At beginning of row ch 3 counts as a dc; ch 4 counts as a tr. At end of row on these designs it is easier to dc in ch-3 sp instead of 3rd ch.

Poinsettias

Filet: Ch 42 loosely.

Row 1: Dc in 4th ch from hook and nxt 2 ch, (ch 2, sk 2 ch, dc in nxt ch) 11 times, dc in nxt 3 ch [= block, 11 sps, block].

Row 2: Ch 3, turn, dc in nxt 3 dc, *(ch 2, dc in nxt dc) 3 times, 2 dc in nxt sp, dc in nxt dc*, rpt from * once more, (ch 2, dc in nxt dc) 3 times, dc in nxt 3 dc [= block, 3 sps, block, 3 sps, block, 3 sps, block].

Row 3: Ch 3, turn, dc in nxt 3 dc, (ch 2, dc in nxt dc) 3 times, dc in nxt 3 dc, 2 dc in sp, dc in nxt dc, ch 2, dc in nxt dc, 2 dc in nxt sp, dc in nxt 4 dc, (ch 2, dc in nxt dc) 3 times, dc in nxt 3 dc [= block, 3 sps, 2 blocks, sp, 2 blocks, 3 sps, block].

Continue with chart and repeat rows 1–4 for a total of 6 motifs. To fasten off, pull thread through loop and leave a long enough thread to whipstitch the first and last rows together.

Scalloped Edging

Row A: Attach thread and sc in end of final row, (ch 12, sc in 5th row, ch 6, sc in 7th row, ch 12, sc in 12th row, ch

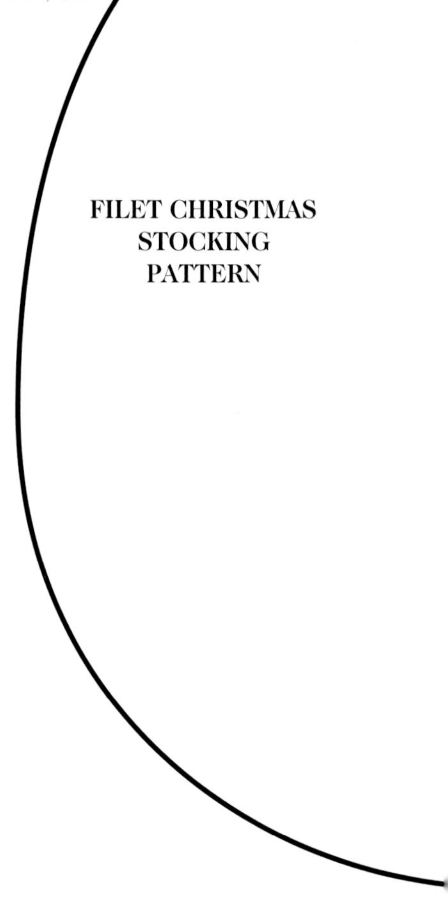

FILET CHRISTMAS STOCKING PATTERN

6, sc in 14th row) around, except instead of final ch 6, make ch 3, dc in first sc.

Row B: (In ch-12 sp make 9 tr, ch 6, sl st in last tr for picot, 9 tr, 2 sc in nxt sp) around, sl st in dc and first tr. Fasten off.

Bows

Filet: Ch 42 loosely.

Row 1: Dc in 4th ch from hook and nxt 2 ch, ch 2, sk 2 ch, dc in nxt 4 ch, (ch 2, sk 2 ch, dc in nxt ch) 2 times, dc in nxt 3 ch, (ch 2, sk 2 ch, dc in nxt ch) 6 times, dc in nxt 3 ch [= block, sp, block, 2 sps, block, 6 sps, block].

Row 2: Ch 3, turn, dc in nxt 3 dc, (ch 2, dc in nxt dc) 6 times, ch 2, sk 2 dc, dc in nxt dc, (ch 2, dc in nxt dc) 2 times, dc in nxt 3 dc, ch 2, dc in nxt 4 dc [= block, 9 sps, block, sp, block].

Row 3: Ch 3, turn, dc in nxt 3 dc, ch 2, dc in nxt 4 dc, (ch 2, dc in nxt dc) 5 times, (2 dc in sp, dc in nxt dc) 2 times, (ch 2, dc in nxt dc) 2 times, dc in nxt 3 dc [= block, sp, block, 5 sps, 2 blocks, 2 sps, block].

Continue with chart and repeat rows 1–4 for a total of 6 motifs. To fasten off, pull thread through loop and leave enough thread to whipstitch the first and last rows together.

Garland Edging

Row A: Attach thread on bottom edge and sc in end of final row. (Ch 4, 3 tr in last sc, ch 4, 3 tr in last tr; ch 6, sl st in last tr for picot, ch 4, 3 tr in same tr, ch 4, 3 tr in last tr; sk 6 rows, sc in nxt row) around, except instead of final sc make sl st in first sc. Fasten off.

To finish filet pieces: Cut thread 2" long and weave in ends. Press if desired, being careful to shape to precise measurements.

Finishing instructions:
Materials:

⅔ yd. 40"-wide burgundy velvet (for front and back stocking pieces)

⅔ yd. 44/45"-wide complementary fabric (for lining)

16" length ¼"-wide complementary ribbon, cut into two 8" pieces (for hanging loops)

Thread to match   Hand-sewing needle

Scissors   Tailor's chalk

Sewing machine (optional)

Note: Materials listed will make two *Filet Christmas Stockings*. Pattern includes a ⅝" seam allowance. Place pattern with toe pointing in direction of your choice, keeping in mind that direction of toe will be reversed when stocking is turned right-side out.

1. Complete crocheted cuffs following instructions given.

2. Cut out pattern.

3. Lay pattern right-side up atop wrong side of velvet, paying close attention to nap of fabric. Pin carefully, using as few pins as possible so as not to mark velvet. Trace around pattern using tailor's chalk, and remove pattern from velvet. Flip pattern and trace a second piece for back of stocking, again paying close attention to nap of fabric. Repeat for second stocking. Repeat for four lining pieces, except place pattern on right side of fabric to trace.

4. Cut out front and back stocking pieces. Pin one front and one back together, placing right sides of fabric together and aligning edges. Sew around perimeter, leaving top of stocking open for turning. Trim seams and turn. Turn top raw edge to inside of stocking and whipstitch in place. Repeat for second stocking. Repeat for lining but do not turn or whipstitch top raw edges.

5. Place lining inside stocking, aligning toe and heel. Turn raw edge of lining under (toward wrong side of velvet) at top of stocking and whipstitch to inside of stocking around top. Whipstitch crocheted cuff around top of stocking, aligning cuff seam with stocking seam. Fold 8" piece ribbon in half to form hanging loop and tack to top of stocking at heel seam. Repeat for second stocking.

Extend pattern 3¾" following illustration below.

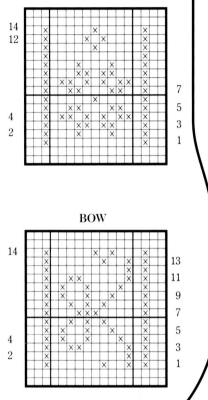

POINSETTIA

BOW

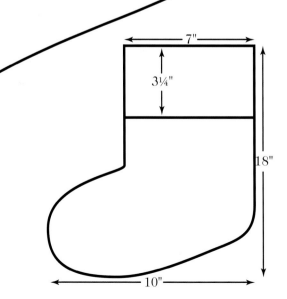

133

Knitted Stocking

Knitting Abbreviations:

co—cast on	rep—repeat
k—knit	sl—slip
nxt—next	st(s)—stitch(es)
p—purl	St st—Stockinette
rem—remaining	stitch

Finished size: 17" from top to toe
Materials:
Caron Wintuk 4-ply 100% Orlon Hand
   Knitting Yarn: One 3.5-oz. skein no. 65
   winter white; small amounts no. 31
   cardinal red and no. 36 spruce
Size 8 knitting needles **or** size needed to
   obtain correct gauge, plus knitting
   needles two sizes smaller
Tapestry needle
Stitch holders
Size 8 double-pointed needles
Gauge: In St st with size 8 needles, 9 sts = 2"

Note: Stocking is worked entirely in stockinette stitch. When shaping heel and toe, "wrap nxt st" means pass yarn to right side of work, sl nxt st to right needle, pass yarn to wrong side of work, return st to left needle.

Instructions: With smaller needles, co 56 sts with winter white. Work in St st for 24 rows. Place markers at each end of last row; this marks top of cuff. Change to larger needles and work in St st for 24 rows; place markers at each end of last row to mark bottom of cuff. Work in St st for 44 rows more, ending with wrong-side row. Cut white.

Heel
Row 1: Sl first 28 sts to holder for instep. With spruce, k rem 28 sts; turn.
Row 2: P 26, wrap nxt st; turn.
Row 3: K 24, wrap nxt st; turn.
Row 4: P 22, wrap nxt st; turn.
Row 5: K 20, wrap nxt st; turn. Continue in this manner, working 2 fewer sts than on previous row before wrapping and turning, to end of row 11.
Row 12: P 6, wrap nxt st; turn.
Row 13: K 6, wrap nxt st; turn.
Row 14: P 8, wrap nxt st; turn.
Row 15: K 10, wrap nxt st; turn. Continue in this manner, working 2 more sts than on previous row before wrapping and turning, to end of row 24.
Row 25: K 28; turn. Cut spruce.

Foot
With winter white, p 28; sl 28 instep sts from holder to right needle and p. Work 56 sts with winter white for 28 rows more, ending with wrong-side row. Cut winter white.

Toe
With cardinal red, k first 28 sts for toe, sl rem 28 foot sts to holder. Shape toe as for heel, ending with row 24 worked as follows: P 28. Weave 28 toe sts to 28 foot sts using Kitchener stitch (see following note) or join and bind off as follows: With 28 foot sts on double-pointed needle and 28 toe sts on second double-pointed needle and with right sides together, k first toe stitch and first instep st together; * k nxt toe and nxt instep together, pass previous st over last st made. Rep from * across. Fasten off.

Note: The Kitchener stitch is sometimes called "weaving the toe." **To work:** Slip toe sts to one double-pointed needle and foot sts to second double-pointed needle. Thread approximately 1 yd. yarn onto tapestry needle. Holding needles parallel with wrong sides of stocking together, with sts at right edge of needles and leaving short tail to be woven in later, * insert tapestry needle into first st of front needle as if to k and sl st off needle; insert tapestry needle into second st of front needle as if to p and draw yarn through, leaving st on needle. Insert tapestry needle into first st on back needle as if to p and remove st from needle, insert tapestry needle into second st on back as if to k and draw yarn through. Rep from * until one st remains on each needle. Draw yarn through st on front needle as if to k and through st on back needle as if to p. Remove double-pointed needles. Weave in ends.

EMBROIDERY
Cuff
With spruce, work 3 evenly spaced rows of herringbone stitch over cuff as follows: Depth of each embroidered row equals 4 knit rows; each herringbone stitch is worked 2 sts to right of and 4 rows above or below previous stitch. Allow 2 knit rows between herringbone rows. With cardinal red, pass needle under each point where herringbone thread crosses itself.

Cross-stitch embroidery:
With cardinal red and spruce, work double cross stitches as shown in illustration, placing stitches randomly between bottom of cuff and top of toe.

To finish:
Fold hem to inside at first set of markers; sew invisibly on inside. Seam stocking. With winter white, make hanging loop at top of hem, directly above center of heel.

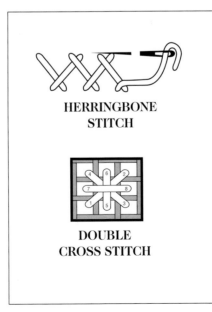

HERRINGBONE STITCH

DOUBLE CROSS STITCH

Woolen Santa Stocking

Materials:
½ yd. 44/45"-wide cream wool flannel
¼ yd. 44/45"-wide teal green wool
   flannel
Scraps of wool flannel, colors: red,
   white, grey
1 skein **each** J. & P. Coats 6-strand embroidery floss, colors: 3019 Rose,
   very deep; 8510 Pearl Grey, very
   dark; 8400 Steel Grey, very
   dark; 6878 Blue Green, dark; 5360 Beige
   Brown, very dark; 3121 Melon, light
1 spool thread, color: cream
12" length ¼"-wide red satin ribbon (for
   hanging loop and bow)
Hand-sewing needle
Scissors
Measuring tape
Iron
Sewing machine with zigzag stitch
   (optional)

1. Enlarge pattern as indicated. Trace stocking pattern onto cream flannel, matching arrows to form whole pattern. **DO NOT CUT OUT.**
2. Transfer appliqué shapes to wool scraps, referring to photo on page 119 for color placement. Cut out shapes. Appliqué around shapes, working a buttonhole stitch around perimeter of each and using two strands matching color of floss.
3. Embroider facial features on Santa, using 3121 for satin-stitched nose, 3019 for backstitched mouth, and 5360 for backstitched eyes. Embroider tree trunk using 5360, taking very narrow satin stitches.
4. Cut stocking shape from flannel ¼" away from markings. Place stocking shape right-side down on right side of

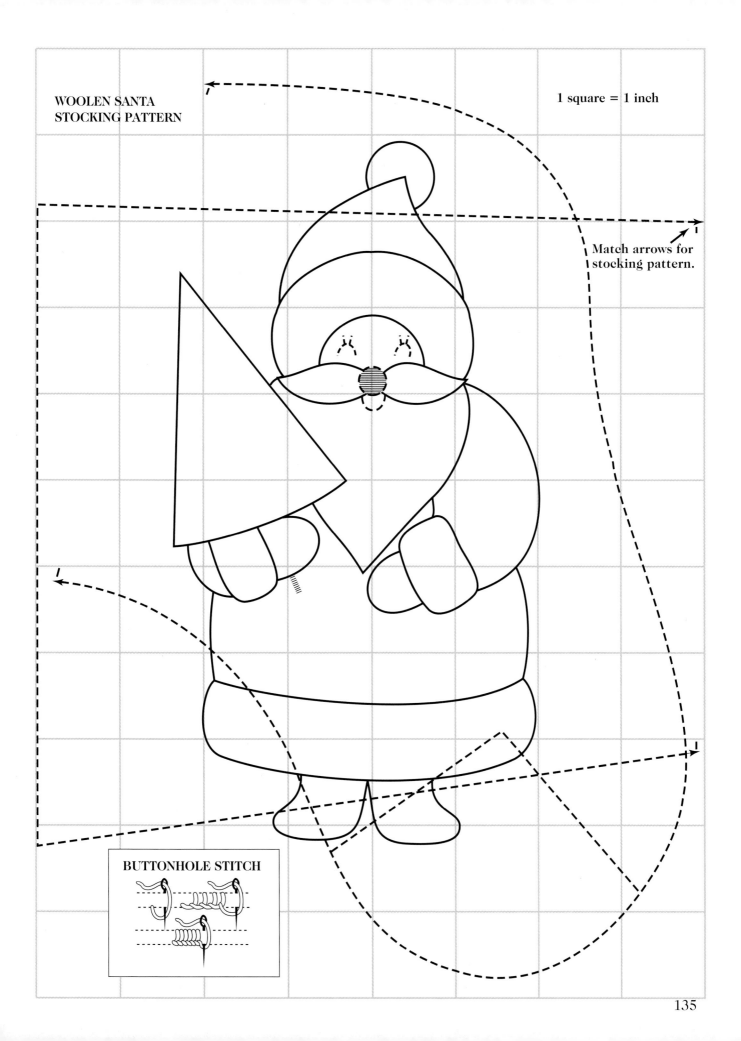

WOOLEN SANTA
STOCKING PATTERN

1 square = 1 inch

Match arrows for
stocking pattern.

BUTTONHOLE STITCH

135

remaining cream flannel. Sew around stocking shape ¼" in from raw edge, leaving top unstitched. Trim excess backing fabric to within ⅛" of stitching line. Overcast or zigzag edges to prevent fraying. Turn stocking right-side out. Press.

5. Cut 5" x 15" strip from teal green flannel for cuff, following straight grain of fabric. Fold strip in half, aligning raw edges of short ends, and sew ends together to form tube, using ¼" seam allowance. Place tube **INSIDE** stocking, having **RIGHT** side of tube against **WRONG** side of stocking and centering tube seam on back of stocking. Sew tube to stocking, using ¼" seam allowance. Turn cuff down to right side of stocking and press. Fringe 1" along lower edge of cuff.

6. Cut one 4" to 5" length from ribbon, bring ends together to form hanging loop, and tack ends inside top of stocking at heel side. Tie a bow in remaining ribbon and tack to outside top of stocking at heel side.

Christmas Log Cabin Quilt

Materials:
⅛ yd. 44/45"-wide red solid fabric (A)
¾ yd. 44/45"-wide white-and-red print fabric (B, C, and inner border)
⅞ yd. 44/45"-wide green print fabric (D and E)
⅞ yd. 44/45"-wide red-and-white print fabric (F and G)
⅞ yd. 44/45"-wide green-and-red print fabric (H and I)
1 yd. 44/45"-wide red print fabric (J and K)
1¼ yd. 44/45"-wide dark green print fabric (L and M)
1 yd. 44/45"-wide dark green solid fabric (for outer border and binding)
1½ yds. 90"-wide complementary fabric, pieced to 47" square (for backing)
47" square lightweight quilt batting
Thread to match fabrics (for piecing and quilting)
Silver marking pencil (for marking quilting designs)
Quilting thread, color: ecru
Hand-sewing needles
Quilting needles   Mechanical pencil
Ruler   Straight pins
Scissors   Iron

Finished size: 47" x 47"
Note: Please read all instructions carefully before beginning. Purchase 100% cotton fabrics. Use a ¼" seam allowance throughout. Illustrations and Quilt Block Assembly Diagram match lower-left quilt block of assembled quilt. Refer to photo on page 120.

1. Cut ¾"-wide strips from white-and-red print fabric for inner border, and piece strips to a length of at least 188". Set aside.
2. Cut 2½"-wide strips from dark green fabric for outer border, and piece strips to a length of at least 188". Set aside.
3. Cut sixteen 2"-square centers from red solid fabric. Set aside.
4. Cut remaining fabrics (except backing fabric) into 2"-wide strips. Assemble quilt blocks as follows, referring to illustrations, following Quilt Block Assembly Diagram for fabric placement, and pressing seams away from center.
5. With right sides of fabric together, sew center square (A) to strip of white-and-red print fabric (B). Press seams. Mark white-and-red print fabric strip 1¾" away from seam and trim.
6. With right sides of fabric together, sew pieces (A) and (B) to strip of white-and-red print fabric (C). Press seams. Trim white-and-red print fabric even with lower edge of fabric (A).
7. Continue piecing in this manner, referring to Quilt Block Assembly Diagram and piecing fabrics in alphabetical order.
8. Assemble sixteen quilt blocks. Piece blocks together, rotating blocks as needed to form pattern on assembled quilt top and referring to photo on page 120 for placement and rotation.
9. Square up quilt.
10. Sew inner border around perimeter of quilt top, mitering at corners. Press. Sew outer border to inner border around perimeter of quilt top, mitering at corners. Press.
11. Layer backing fabric right-side down, batting, and assembled quilt top right-side up atop a flat surface, aligning edges. Pin or baste through all layers. Quilt in the seams, using thread to match fabrics. Remove pins or basting threads.
12. To make binding, cut 1½"-wide strips from remaining dark green solid fabric, and piece together to a length of at least 208". Fold strip in half along lengthwise edge with wrong sides together and attach around perimeter of quilt front, aligning raw edges. Sew binding to quilt, mitering at each corner. Cut off excess binding and turn ends under to finish neatly. Turn binding to back of quilt and blind stitch in place.
13. Trace holly and bell motif onto outer border, using silver marking pencil. (Note: Four motifs will fit on each side with bell and two holly leaves placed diagonally in corners.) Quilt using ecru thread.
14. Be sure to sign and date the back of your quilt, with either a permanent pen or with embroidery stitches.

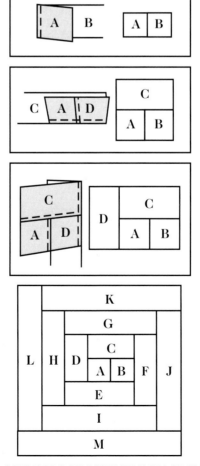

QUILT BLOCK ASSEMBLY DIAGRAM

Christmas Log Cabin Stocking

Materials:

⅛ yd. 44/45"-wide green print fabric (for center squares)

⅜ yd. **each** three **different** 44/45"-green print fabrics (for strips)

⅜ yd. **each** three **different** 44/45"-red print fabrics (for strips)

⅓ yd. 44/45"-wide complementary fabric (for backing)

⅓ yd. 44/45"-wide complementary fabric (for lining)

10" x 20" piece lightweight quilt batting

7" length ¼"-wide red satin ribbon (for hanging loop)

Thread to match fabrics (for piecing)

Quilting thread, color: ecru

Hand-sewing needles Quilting needles
Ruler Straight pins
Scissors Iron

Note: Please read all instructions carefully before beginning. Purchase 100% cotton fabrics. Use a ¼" seam allowance throughout.

1. Cut eleven 2" square centers from green print fabric. Set aside.

2. Cut remaining fabrics (except backing and lining fabric) into 1"-wide strips.

3. Assemble blocks as for *Log Cabin Quilt*, referring to Quilt Block Assembly Diagram for color placement. Assemble completed blocks as shown in Illustration A.

4. Layer lining fabric right-side down, batting, and stocking front right-side up atop a flat surface. Pin or baste through all layers. Quilt ¼" away from seams. Remove pins or basting threads.

5. Cut out stocking pattern and place right-side up atop right side of quilted stocking front. Trace around pattern. Cut out stocking shape. Repeat for backing fabric, placing backing fabric wrong-side up.

6. Place stocking front and back with right sides together and sew together around edges, leaving top of stocking open for turning. Turn stocking right-side out. Turn top of stocking under ½", turn raw edge under, and sew in place.

7. Bring ribbon ends together to form hanging loop and tack ends inside top of stocking at heel side.

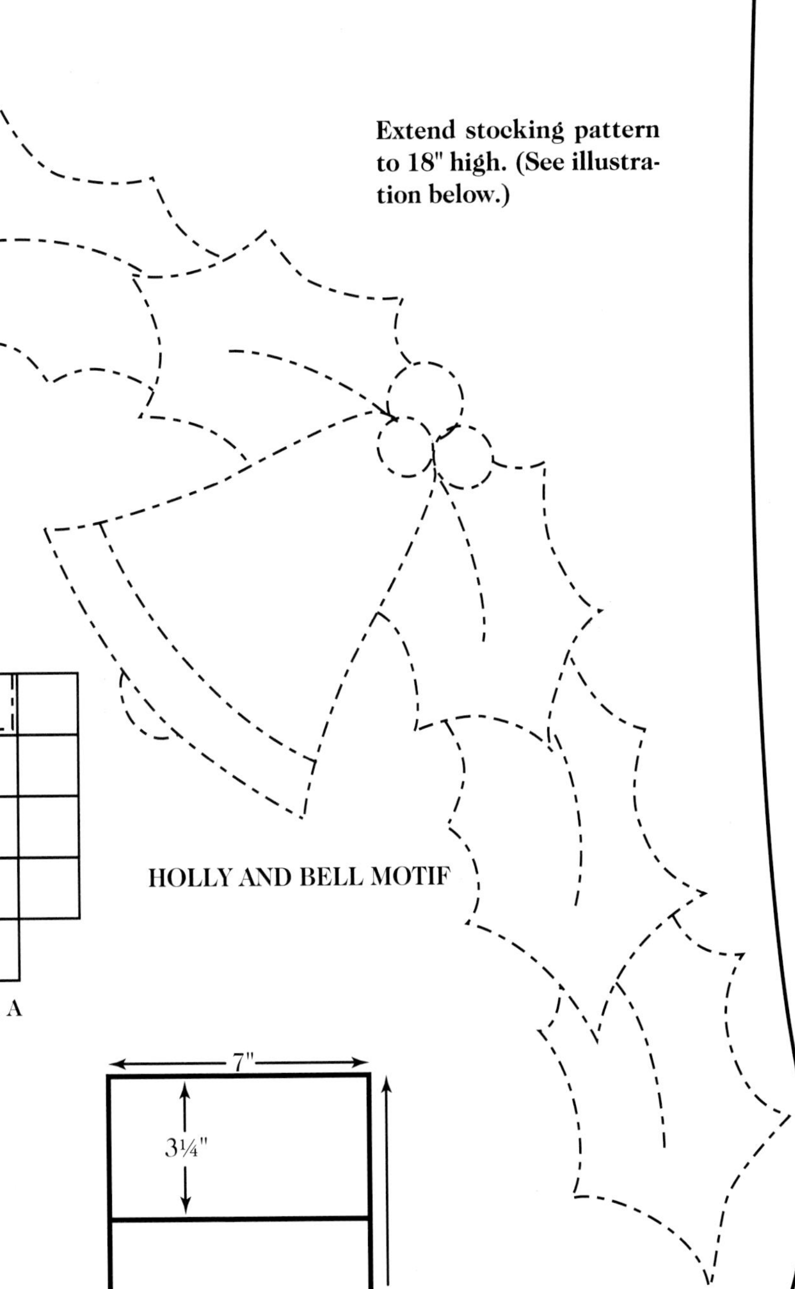

Extend stocking pattern to 18" high. (See illustration below.)

ILL. A

HOLLY AND BELL MOTIF

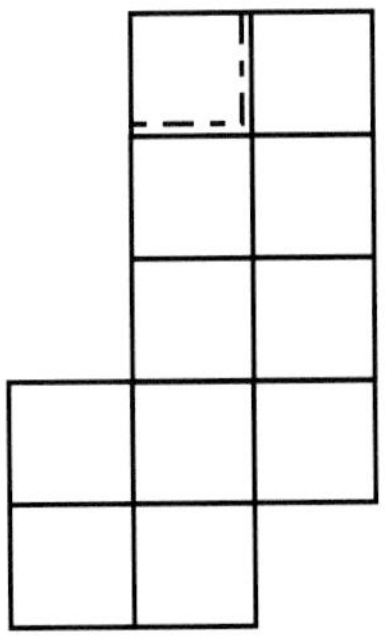

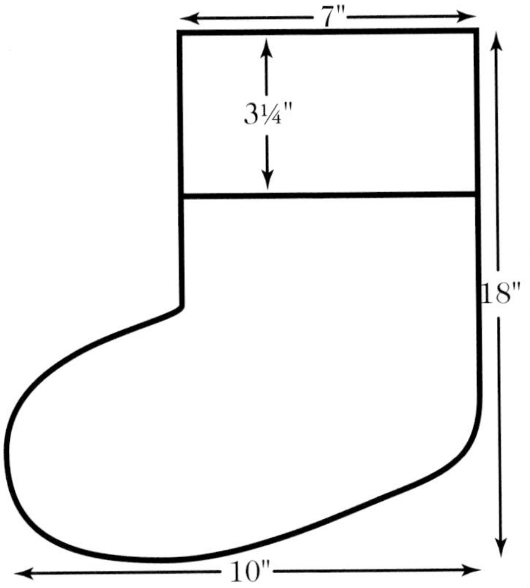

"Frosty" Wall Hanging

Materials:

1 yd. 44/45"-wide red print fabric
½ yd. 44/45"-wide pale blue print **or** solid fabric
½ yd. 44/45"-wide white solid fabric
¼ yd. 44/45"-wide green solid fabric
Small scraps of black and orange fabrics
¾ yd. 44/45"-wide lightweight quilt batting
1 yd. tear-away stabilizer **or** freezer paper
½ yd. fusible web
1 pkg. Coats Extra Wide Double Fold Bias Tape, Art. M. 890, color: 177 Kerry Green
1 spool **each** Coats Rayon Machine Embroidery Thread, Art. D. 63, colors: 12 Black, 135C Tango, 3 Ciel, 177 Kerry Green
1 spool **each** Coats Dual Duty Plus Thread, Art. 210, colors: 01 White, 177 Kerry Green
1 spool Coats Clear Nylon Monofilament
Water-soluble fabric-marking pen
Scissors
Sewing machine with zigzag stitch
Iron

Note: Please read all instructions carefully before beginning. Purchase 100% cotton fabrics. Use a ¼" seam allowance throughout. Press all seam allowances toward darker fabrics to avoid shadows.

1. Enlarge pattern pieces as indicated. Cut out.

2. Trace four stars and one of **each** remaining pattern piece onto paper side of fusible web. Fuse snowman and stars to white solid, circles to black print, and nose to orange print, following manufacturer's instructions for fusing. Fuse main portion of hat to green solid and hatband to red print. Cut out shapes along solid lines. Do not cut on any dotted lines.

3. Cut four 5" squares and one 15½" x 21½" rectangle from blue fabric. Fuse one star to center of each 5" square. Fuse snowman to center of rectangle. Lightly mark areas indicated by dotted lines onto snowman body, using water-soluble fabric-marking pen. Fuse remaining appliqué pieces to snowman, aligning hat brim with line indicated at top of snowman's head. Pin or baste stabilizer to back side of **each** blue fabric piece.

Note: If using freezer paper, iron to back side of blue fabric pieces.

4. Load machine and bobbin with Ciel thread. Set machine to a narrow machine satin stitch and appliqué stars and snowman's body to background fabrics. Stitch into areas indicated by marked lines, tapering ends to form points.

Note: Appliqué stars onto blocks so that tops of stars point in same direction.

5. Using like-colored thread in both machine and bobbin, appliqué snowman's nose using Tango, circles using Black, and hat using Kerry Green.

6. Cut four 2" x 21½" strips and four 2" x 15½" strips from red print. Cut two 2" x 21½" strips and two 2" x 15½" strips from green solid. Load white thread in machine and bobbin and, using a straight stitch, attach a long red strip to each side of long green strip along lengthwise edges, referring to photo on page 121. Repeat for second long set of green and red strips and for shorter sets of strips to form two long and two short strip units. Sew one star block to each short end of the two short strip units, placing star blocks so that

tops of stars are pointing in same direction.

7. Sew one long strip unit to each side of snowman rectangle. Sew shorter strip units with star blocks to top and bottom of snowman rectangle. Press.

8. Cut a 30" x 36" piece from red print fabric for backing.

9. Layer backing right-side down, batting, and assembled quilt top right-side up atop a flat surface. Pin or baste layers together.

10. Load top of machine with Clear Nylon Monofilament, leaving white thread in bobbin. Machine quilt along all seam lines and around appliqué shapes. Quilt "snow drifts" in open areas to sides of snowman. Remove pins or basting threads.

11. Square up quilt. Bind quilt with Extra Wide Double Fold Bias Tape, using Kerry Green thread.

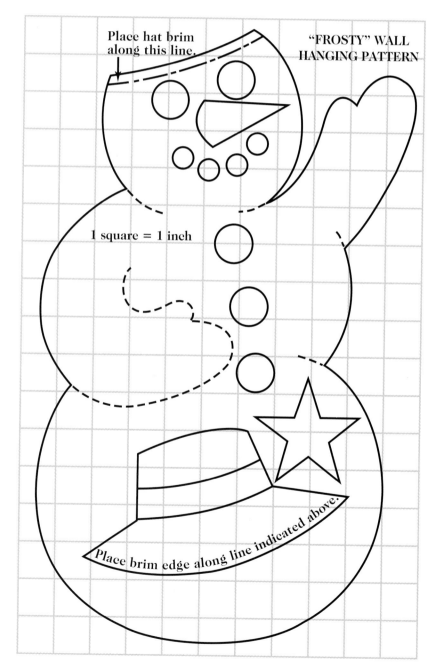

Place hat brim along this line.

"FROSTY" WALL HANGING PATTERN

1 square = 1 inch

Place brim edge along line indicated above.

Tangled Lights

Materials:

2½ yds. 44/45"-wide white broadcloth

¼ yd. 44/45"-wide black broadcloth

½ yd. **total** of brightly colored solid scraps, colors: red, blue, yellow, light green, dark green, aqua, orange

3 pkgs. Coats Soutache Braid, Art. M. 10, color: 2 Black

2 pkgs. Coats Extra Wide Double Fold Bias Tape, Art. M. 890, color: 9 Yale Blue

1 spool **each** Coats Dual Duty Plus thread, Art. 210, colors 1 White, 2 Black, 9 Yale Blue

1 spool **each** Coats Rayon Machine Embroidery Thread, Art. D. 63, colors: 2 Black, 128 Red, 9 Yale Blue, 177 Kerry Green, 287A Bright Green, 182 Spark Gold, 96 Violet, 135C Tango

¾ yd. fusible web

22" x 36" piece lightweight quilt batting

Water-soluble fabric-marking pen

Scissors   Iron

Sewing machine with zigzag stitch

Note: Please read all instructions carefully before beginning. Purchase 100% cotton fabrics. Use a ¼" seam allowance throughout.

Banner

1. Cut one 19" x 32" rectangle from white broadcloth for banner front. Fold in quarters to find center. Mark. Enlarge *WELCOME* letters as indicated and trace, placing letter patterns right side up on paper side of fusible web. Letters will be backward on fusible web. This is correct, and letter patterns should be used with their right sides up as the process for fusing will reverse the fabric designs from the way they appear on the paper patterns. Cut out. Center letters on white broadcloth rectangle, placing top left edge of *W* 4½" from left side of rectangle and leaving approximately ⅛" space between each letter. Fuse letters to white broadcloth rectangle, following manufacturer's instructions for fusing. (**Note:** Right edge of second *E* will be approximately 4¼" from right side of rectangle.) Machine appliqué letters using red thread and a narrow (⅛"-wide) satin stitch.

2. With water-soluble fabric-marking pen, freehand placement line for light string, referring to photo on page 122, making sure loops are approximately 3" wide, and staying at least 1" from sides of rectangle. Straight stitch braid along pencil line, using black thread.

3. Trace nineteen lights and nineteen light caps onto fusible web. Fuse caps to black broadcloth and lights to assorted bright solids. Cut out. Arrange lights on banner along braid, placing one light cap over one end of braid. Fuse in place. Machine appliqué as for letters, using thread to match each light. Appliqué one black cap to each light, using black thread. Trace plug end onto fusible web and fuse to black broadcloth. Cut out. Fuse plug end over remaining end of braid and machine appliqué using black thread. To make plug teeth, machine satin stitch two ⅜"-long lines at straight edge of plug, referring to photo for placement.

4. Cut one 22" x 36" rectangle from white broadcloth for backing. Lay quilt batting atop backing and center banner front right-side up atop batting. Pin or baste layers together. Machine quilt along braid, using black thread, and around lettering, using red thread. Trim excess batting and backing and bind edges, using one package bias tape and blue thread.

Table Center Square

1. Cut one 44" square from remaining white broadcloth.

2. Mark lines for braid in same manner as for banner. Machine stitch braid using black thread.

3. Trace forty-three lights and forty-three light caps onto fusible web. Fuse light shapes to bright solids and caps to black broadcloth. Trace one plug end onto fusible web and fuse to black broadcloth. Cut out. Arrange lights along braid. Machine appliqué as for banner. Repeat for caps and plug end.

4. Bind tablecloth using remaining bias tape and blue thread.

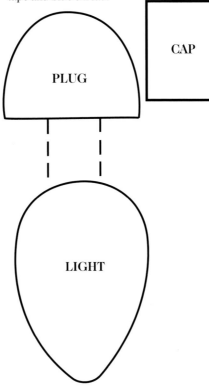

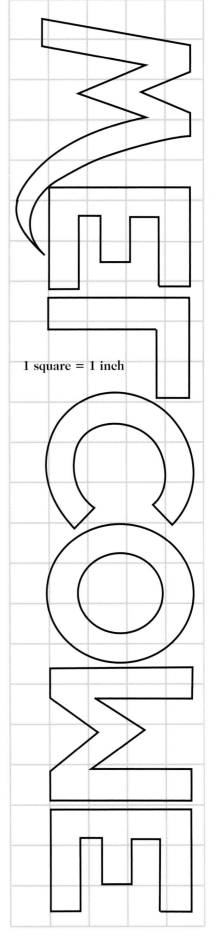

1 square = 1 inch

Cathedral Window Quilt

Materials:
½ yd. 44/45"-wide green print fabric
1½ yds. 44/45"-wide red solid fabric
3 yds. 44/45"-wide muslin
Small scraps fabric, colors: yellow **or** gold, brown
7"-square piece cardboard
2"-square piece cardboard
Thread to match muslin
Hand-sewing needle   Measuring tape
Pencil   Scissors   Iron

Finished size: 42" x 42"
Note: Please read all instructions carefully before beginning. Purchase 100% cotton fabrics.

1. Cut eighty-two 2" squares from green fabric, two-hundred twenty-nine 2" squares from red fabric, two 2" squares from brown fabric, one 2" square from yellow or gold fabric, and one hundred sixty-six 7" squares from muslin.
2. Find center of each 7" square by measuring in from sides, or by folding. Mark. Press in ¼" hem on all sides, referring to Illustration 1. Fold each corner to center mark and press folds, referring to Illustration 2 and making sure that each corner comes to a sharp point. Fold corners to center again, pressing each fold. When all corners have been folded and pressed twice, tack points in center, referring to Illustration 3.

3. Butt edges of folded squares together, referring to Illustration 4, and zigzag or whipstitch them together into blocks of four, referring to Illustration 5. Zigzag or whipstitch blocks together in rows.
Note: This *Cathedral Window Quilt* requires thirteen rows of thirteen blocks.
4. To fill windows, begin in center of quilt and place 2" fabric square over each seam, referring to Illustration 5 and placing colors as indicated in Illustration 6. Fold edges of muslin over each square and appliqué fold, referring to Illustration 5.

Snowflake Quilt

Materials:
¾ yd. 44/45"-wide white fabric
½ yd. 44/45"-wide light red print fabric
¾ yd. 44/45"-wide dark red print fabric
1 yd. 44/45"-wide complementary fabric (for backing)
31" square lightweight quilt batting
Thread to match fabrics (for piecing)
Quilting thread, colors: red, white
Plastic **or** paper (for templates)
Mechanical pencil
Silver marking pencil (for marking quilting designs)
¼"-wide masking tape (for marking quilting designs)
Measuring tape   Hand-sewing needles
Quilting needles   Straight pins
Scissors
Iron

Finished Size: 27" x 27"
Note: Please read all instructions carefully before beginning. Purchase 100% cotton fabrics. Use a ¼" seam allowance throughout.

1. To conserve fabric, cut borders first. Cut four 30" x 1½" strips from light red print fabric. Cut four 30" x 3" strips from white fabric. Cut four 30" x 2½" strips from dark red print fabric. Cut three 44" x 2½" strips from dark red print fabric for binding.
2. Trace around all pattern pieces on plastic or paper to make templates. Cut out.
3. Draw around templates on back side of fabric, using mechanical pencil for narrow line and leaving at least ½" space between each piece to allow for ¼" seam allowance. Cut fabric pieces as follows:
  Template 1: twelve from white
  Template 2: eight from white
  Template 3: four from white
  Template 4: twelve from light red print
  Template 4: twenty from dark red print
4. Piece center star by joining eight red diamonds (*Template 4*), alternating dark and light red print fabrics. Set in eight white squares (*Template 1*) around star.
5. Piece the four outer partial stars by joining four dark red and two light red diamonds for each, referring to photo on page 124 for placement. Set in one white square and two white triangles (*Template 2*) to each partial star.
6. Set in each partial star to one corner of center star, referring to photo. Complete snowflake design by setting in one white rectangle (*Template 3*) on each side of design.
7. To make borders, sew together one light red print fabric strip, one white fabric strip, and one dark red print fabric strip. Pin strips to each side of snowflake design, centering strip so that equal amounts of fabric extend from each side. Sew the four border strips in place, being sure to start and stop each stitching line ¼" from each outside edge. Carefully miter each corner. Press quilt top lightly.
8. Trace quilting design on paper and cut out. (**Note:** Make your own snowflake quilting design by folding a 2½" square of paper into quarters and cutting desired design.) Lightly transfer snowflake design onto white squares, rectangles, and along border, using silver marking pencil. Use ¼" masking tape as a guide for quilting around each red diamond.
9. Layer backing fabric right-side down, batting, and completed quilt top right-side up atop a flat surface. Pin. Baste through all layers. Remove pins.
10. Quilt along marked design on white fabric pieces. Quilt around diamonds,

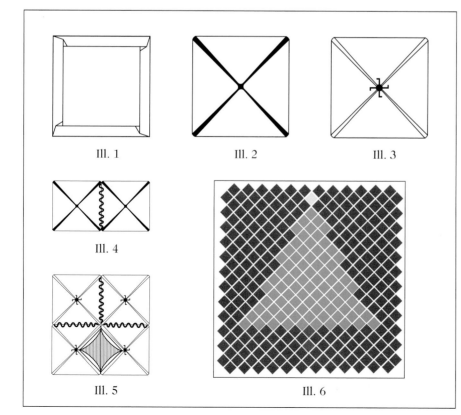

Ill. 1   Ill. 2   Ill. 3

Ill. 4

Ill. 5   Ill. 6

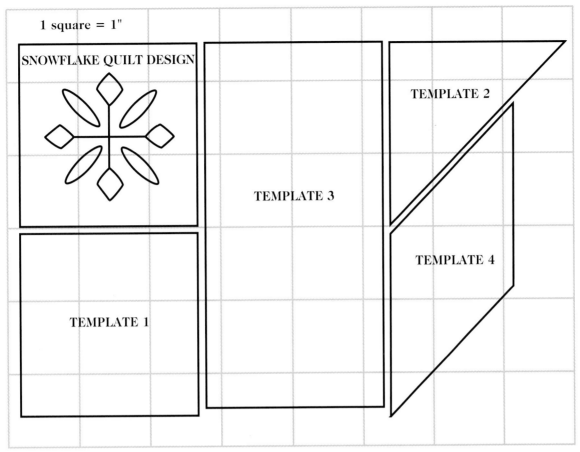

SNOWFLAKE QUILT DESIGN

TEMPLATE 2

TEMPLATE 3

TEMPLATE 4

TEMPLATE 1

using small quilting needle and thread to match fabric pieces and taking small running stitches through all layers.

11. Square up quilt.

12. To make binding, sew 2½"-wide dark red print fabric strips together to a length of at least 116". Fold strip in half along lengthwise edge with wrong sides together and attach around perimeter of quilt front, aligning raw edges. Sew binding to quilt, using ¼" seam allowance and mitering at each corner. Cut off excess binding and turn under ends to finish neatly. Turn binding to back of quilt and blind stitch in place.

13. Be sure to sign and date the back of your quilt, with either a permanent pen or with embroidery stitches. If you wish to hang your quilt for display, add a sleeve for a dowel or attach a curtain ring for hanging at each top corner.

Stitch Diagrams

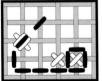

Backstitch (across two ¾ stitches and around full cross)

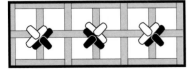

¾ Cross Stitches (over one in various positions)

Full Cross Stitch (over one thread)

¼ Cross Stitch (over one thread)

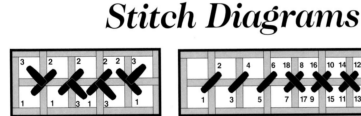

Two ¾ Stitches (in one square, using two different floss colors)

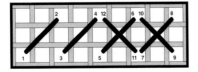

Full Cross Stitch (over two threads)

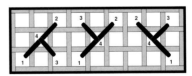

¾ Cross Stitch (over two threads)

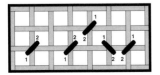

¼ Cross Stitch (over two threads)

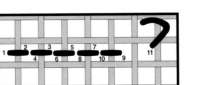

Basic Backstitch

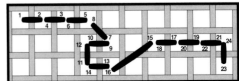

Backstitch (showing variations)

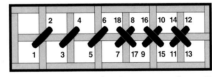
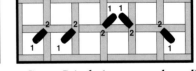

141

General Instructions for Cross Stitch

Basic Supplies: Even-weave fabric, tapestry needle(s), six-strand embroidery floss, embroidery scissors, embroidery hoop (optional).

Fabric Preparation: The instructions and yardage for finishing materials have been written and calculated for each of the projects shown stitched on the fabric listed in each color code. Alternate fabric choices have also been listed. If you wish to stitch a design on an alternate fabric, or alter its placement, you will need to recalculate the finished size of the project, as well as the yardage of finishing materials needed, and make the necessary dimension adjustments when finishing.

Determine size of fabric needed for a project by dividing number of horizontal stitches by thread count of fabric. For example, if a design 35 stitches wide is worked on 14-count fabric, it will cover 2½" (35 divided by 14 equals 2½). Repeat process for vertical count. Add three inches on all sides of design area to find dimensions for cutting fabric. Whipstitch edges to prevent fraying.

Floss Preparation: Cut floss into 14" to 18" lengths. Separate all six strands. Reunite number of strands needed and thread needle, leaving one floss end longer than the other.

Where to Start: Start wherever you like! Some designers suggest finding center of fabric and starting there. Others recommend beginning with a central motif, while still others work borders first. Many find fabric center, count up and back to the left, and start with the uppermost left stitch. Wherever you begin, be sure to leave allowance for all horizontal and vertical stitches so that a 3" fabric margin is left around completed design.

Should you choose to begin at the center point, find it by folding fabric from top to bottom and then from left to right. Use a straight pin to mark upper-left corner at junction of folds, and then unfold fabric. Pin will be in center of fabric.

After deciding where to begin on fabric, find same point on graph. Each square on graph represents one stitch. Those squares containing a symbol (i.e., X,T,O) indicate that a stitch should be made in that space over those threads. Different symbols represent different colors of floss for stitches. (See color code of chart.) They may also indicate partial or decorative stitches. Familiarize yourself with color code before you begin stitching. Even-weave fabric may be stretched over an embroidery hoop to facilitate stitching.

Stitching the Design: Using the illustrations on page 142, stitch design, completing all full and partial cross stitches first. Cross all full cross stitches in same direction to achieve a smooth surface appearance. Work backstitches second, and any decorative stitches last.

Helpful Hints for Stitching: Do not knot floss. Instead, catch end on back of work with first few stitches. As you stitch, pull floss through fabric "holes" with one stroke, not several short ones. The moment you feel resistance from floss, cease pulling. Consistent tension on floss results in a smoother look for stitches. Drop your needle frequently to allow floss to untwist. It twists naturally as you stitch and, as it gets shorter, must be allowed to untwist more often. To begin a new color on project, prepare floss and secure new strands as noted. To end stitching, run floss under several completed stitches and clip remaining strands close to surface. Many times it is necessary to skip a few spaces (threads) on the fabric in order to continue a row of stitches in the same color. If you must skip an area covering more than ¼", end stitching as described and begin again at next point. This procedure prevents uneven tension on the embroidery surface and snagging on back. It also keeps colors from showing through unstitched areas. Do not carry thread over an area that will remain unstitched.

When You Are Finished: For designs using cotton or linen floss on cotton or linen even-weave fabric, hand wash piece with mild detergent in warm water. Rinse thoroughly with cold water. Roll in terry towel and squeeze gently to remove excess moisture. Do not wring. Unroll towel and allow piece to dry until barely damp. Iron on padded surface with design face down, using medium setting for heat. A press cloth will help prevent shine on dark fabrics. **Note:** Acrylics, acrylic blends, wools or silks must be treated differently when cleaning. Check manufacturer's guidelines for special cleaning instructions.

Helpful Hints for Crafting

The instructions and yardage for finishing materials have been written and calculated for each of the projects shown and crafted from the materials listed. If you wish to craft a design using materials of different dimensions than those listed or to stitch a design on an alternate fabric or to alter its placement, you will need to recalculate the finished size of the project, as well as the yardage of finishing materials needed, and make the necessary dimension adjustments when purchasing supplies and making the projects. For general instructions for making a bow, refer to page 129.

Crafters and Designers

Shopper's Guide

Redware Hearts Ornaments
Page 10—Sculpey clay available from Aardvark Adventures, Post Office Box, 2449, Livermore, CA 94551.

Music Room Tree
Page 17—Beethoven bust from Waccamaw, Birmingham, Alabama.

Christmas Rabbit and Bear
Page 41—Floral pillow from Linens 'N Things, 116 Riverchase Village, Birmingham, AL 35216; floral hangers from Rich's, Birmingham, Alabama.

Elegant Pillows
Page 42—Brass urn from Waccamaw, Birmingham, Alabama.

As Ye Sew Pillow
Page 46—Lift-N-Snip® scissors from Hoffman Distributing Company, Inc., 5501 Highway 280 East, Suite 102, Leeds, AL 35094, 1-800-624-8866.

French Horn
Page 47—Mill Hill Glass Pebble Beads available from Gay Bowles Sales, Inc.

Victorian Sleigh
Page 50—Gold-trimmed ribbon from The Ritz Florist, 4647-E Highway 280, Birmingham, AL 35242.

Three Carolers
Page 52—Gold bells and all ribbons from Smith Variety, 2715 Culver Road, Mountain Brook, AL 35223.

Trio of Centerpiece Trees
Page 72—Orange bowls from Pier 1 Imports, Birmingham, Alabama; pink Christmas balls from The Ritz Florist, 4647-E Highway 280, Birmingham, AL 35242.

Fun Felt Trees
Page 78—Felt and assorted confetti from Michael's Arts & Crafts, Birmingham, Alabama; boys' red sweater and green

cotton shirt courtesy of McRae's, Birmingham, Alabama.

Musical Instruments Place Mats
Page 82—China pattern is Melina by Villeroy and Boch.

Christmas Wreath Sweater
Page 105—Red-and-white striped sweater (#292, $29.50 plus $3.75 shipping and handling—M, L, XL, XXL) from Just CrossStitch®, 405 Riverhills Business Park, Birmingham, AL 35242, 1-800-768-5878.

"Frosty" Wall Hanging
Page 121—Bear was crafted from an old chenille bedspread using Simplicity pattern #7210.

Items not appearing in "Shopper's Guide" are either commonly available, antiques, or from private collections.

Index